College Professors and
Their Impact on Students

College Professors and Their Impact on Students

ROBERT C. WILSON
JERRY G. GAFF

Evelyn R. Dienst
Lynn Wood
James L. Bavry

A WILEY-INTERSCIENCE PUBLICATION

John Wiley & Sons

New York • London • Sydney • Toronto

033977

Copyright © 1975, by John Wiley & Sons, Inc.

All rights reserved. Published simultaneously in Canada.

No part of this book may be reproduced by any means, nor transmitted, nor translated into a machine language without the written permission of the publisher.

Library of Congress Cataloging in Publication Data

Wilson, Robert Charles, 1920–
    College professors and their impact on students.

    "A Wiley-Interscience publication."
    Includes index.
    1. College teaching.   2. Teacher-student relationships.   I. Title.

LB2331.W53   378.1′2   74-26553
ISBN 0-471-94961-2

Printed in the United States of America

10 9 8 7 6 5 4 3 2

Foreword

Ted Newcomb was recently quoted as saying "What does college do for a person? Frankly very little. There isn't, I'm afraid, much evidence that faculty *do* have any effect on students. The fact is that students neither expect much faculty contact nor get it. In most colleges, the faculty goes one way and the students go another." *

As soon as I finish writing this foreword I shall send this manuscript to Ted, for Wilson, Gaff, and their colleagues have shown that on a variety of types of campuses some students seek out faculty and faculty derive great satisfaction from interactions with students. And not only is the relationship satisfying, it also has an impact on the student's cognitive and affective development.

In a nice convergent methodology using test scores, students' perceptions of impact, faculty members' own perceptions of their impact, and colleague ratings of the faculty members whom they regard as most impactful Wilson and Gaff identify professors who interact with students frequently and effectively.

This book provides a nice balance of empirical data from two major studies with generalizations and suggestions useful to students, faculty, administrators and all those who hope to help prove Ted Newcomb's pessimism untrue.

Knowing Ted's optimism and energy I suspect that he, as he has all his life, will be out in front leading those using the insights derived from this book to make colleges and universities truly educational.

Wilbert J. McKeachie

Ann Arbor, Michigan
August 1974

* *Psychology Today*, September 1974, p. 73.

Preface

This is a book about college teachers, college teaching, and college students. It is intended to be in part a report of empirical research, in part a book that raises issues for discussion, in part an information guide in that it includes examples of existing efforts to improve teaching.

The two research studies that provide the empirical basis of the book were conducted by the authors while they were members of the Center for Research and Development in Higher Education at the University of California, Berkeley. The studies were part of a larger program at the Center designed to study how various aspects of the college experience affect student development and change.

Earlier studies at the Center and elsewhere using data from students seemed to indicate that for most students, teachers and teaching were not major agents of influence, even in their intellectual development. The great majority of students expressed a desire for more personal contacts with teachers, yet most of them indicated that they had become personally acquainted with only one or two faculty members while in college. Only a small minority of students indicated that one or more teachers had been instrumental in a major decision or in giving new direction to their lives.

Many people, of course, questioned the validity of these rather pessimistic findings about the effects of college teachers. The conviction that college teachers, at least *some* college teachers, do make a difference led us to search for new ways to address the question. The purpose of our research was to pursue the issue in more depth using data from faculty as well as from students and using measures of student change and development over a four-year period. The general research question we set out to address was: "What are the ways in which different kinds of faculty members influence or fail to influence different kinds of students?"

To pursue an answer to this question we needed to decide on ways to characterize college teachers and ways to characterize students. We also needed ways of examining those variables that seemed likely to be important determiners of the influence or impact of college teachers on at least some of their students.

At the time our studies were initiated there was very little descriptive data available on what college and university faculty members were like. Particularly lacking were data from faculty members themselves about their attitudes, values, activities, and teaching practices.

To assist us in deciding on the most promising ways of characterizing college teachers, the first study was conducted in 1968 using data from 1000 faculty members at six colleges and universities. The institutions were deliberately selected for their diversity to maximize the possibilities of discovering the range of faculty characteristics that might be useful in differentiating among different kinds of teachers.

The data from this first study provided many interesting findings about the characteristics of college and university teachers that are related to their views of teaching, students, and educational change. It also helped us to hypothesize about the kinds of faculty characteristics that might be most important to pursue in the second study.

The problem of characterizing students was somewhat simpler. There already existed an extensive body of research findings about the diversity of college students' abilities, attitudes, values, and activities. The researchers at the Center who were conducting two longitudinal studies of student development were building on this knowledge base. They already had many leads as to the variables most likely to be important in characterizing students and in examining significant aspects of their undergraduate education.

Drawing on the results of the first study of faculty and on the longitudinal research on students, we designed the second study to obtain information from both faculty and students at eight colleges and universities. The students were seniors at the time of the study. This made it possible for us to relate information from faculty about their teaching to information from students about their learning experiences and outcomes. Among the topics explored in this study are the characteristics of effective teachers, academic experiences and changes of students having different patterns of interests, qualities of potent faculty–student relationships, factors associated with intellectual development of students, effects of out-of-class interaction for students and faculty, and the effects of college settings on both teaching and learning.

Because we were concerned from the outset with the value and utility of this research for educators "in the field," we have chosen to address our findings to the large group of persons who share a concern and a responsibility for improving college education—teachers, students, administrators, trustees, legislators, and the informed public. In the interest of communicating effectively with these persons, the use of specialized jargon, extended methodological discussion, and treatment of technical issues has been minimized as far as possible.

To increase the usefulness of the book to this group we have included in our discussions extrapolations from the data and also examples and suggestions for the improvement of teaching and learning. Since the amount of research in this area is limited, many of the findings and interpretations must be treated as first approximations. The reader is encouraged to generate alternative explanations and implications.

If the pages that follow help others to better understand college and university professors and facilitate in some small way the actual improvement of teaching and learning, we shall be gratified.

ACKNOWLEDGMENTS

The research on which much of this book is based was supported by the Office of Education, U. S. Department of Health, Education and Welfare. We would like to acknowledge the encouragement and intellectual stimulation of our many colleagues at the Center for Research and Development in Higher Education. We are particularly grateful to Paul Heist, David Whittaker, Mildred Henry, Sarah Cirese, and Jeff Koon who worked cooperatively with us, gave us access to their longitudinal data on students and enabled us to look at the educational process from both faculty and student viewpoints.

Some of the findings in this volume are based on our previously published articles. We wish to thank the publishers of *The Sociology of Education, Change,* and *The Journal of Higher Education* for permission to use the copyrighted materials included in Chapters 4, 5, and 6, respectively.

To the many colleagues who read earlier drafts of the manuscript go our thanks for their helpful suggestions and to our editors at the Center, Harriet Renaud and Jack Warner, our thanks for their creative assistance and patient attention to detail.

We are also indebted to our external advisory committee which gave us advice and encouragement through the course of our research. The members of the committee were Jack Block, University of California, Berkeley; Wilbert McKeachie, University of Michigan; and Leona Tyler, University of Oregon.

Finally, our thanks to the several thousand faculty members and students who provided the data on which the studies are based.

Robert C. Wilson
Jerry G. Gaff
Evelyn R. Dienst
Lynn Wood
James L. Bavry

Berkeley, California
August 1974

Contents

College Professors and
Their Impact on Students

STUDY I

Faculty Views
of Teaching

ROBERT C. WILSON
JERRY G. GAFF

Evelyn R. Dienst
Lynn Wood
James L. Bavry

Chapter 1

Why Study
College Professors?

American higher education is emerging from the most turbulent era in its history. It has been subjected to a lack of public trust; it has been caught up in a myriad of social changes; and it has been charged with the task of serving a more diverse student population than has been its custom. During the 1960s, higher education also experienced unparallelled growth in all facets of its operation. These several changes have resulted in increased access to college not only for highly motivated, middle-class, white students but also for youth from ethnic minorities and from less affluent backgrounds. Although the problem of providing wide access to college is not yet fully solved, the need to provide effective instruction for a wide variety of students has become central.

The broadening base of undergraduate education has called into question the relevancy of traditional liberal arts and university curricula, established professor–student role relationships, and the usual modes of college and university instruction. Nor has all of the current questioning of traditional higher education been initiated by or on behalf of "new" students. Much of the student turmoil of the late 1960s was created by middle-class students in the interest of changing higher education to become more responsive to social needs, to create more humanitarian environments, and to adopt more democratic systems of governance. Of all the concerns for higher education, however, perhaps the strongest—and most unifying—is the sense of an urgent need to make teaching a more central function of college and university faculty and to raise the quality of instruction in all institutions of higher education.

Proposals that underline the need to increase the importance of teaching as well as to effect significant changes in its form and content have been advanced from many quarters in recent years. Prestigious national commissions have echoed campus radicals in calling for greater emphasis on teaching, more socially relevant curricula, closer student–faculty relationships, and greater student participation in formulating institutional policies. The Carnegie Commission on Higher Education (1971), the Assembly on University Goals and Governance (1971), and the Task Force on Academic Reform of the U.S. Department of Health, Education and Welfare (1971) have all issued reports recommending major changes in the organization and operation of colleges and universities. The Fund for the Improvement of Postsecondary Education has been established at the federal level to provide financial support for reforms in postsecondary institutions. All of these efforts involve altering the traditional activities of teachers and the relationships between faculty and students. It is important to recognize, therefore, that if any of these proposals are to be successfully implemented, they will require the consent and support of faculty members themselves.

How likely is it that this consent and support will be forthcoming? Despite the acknowledged importance of college professors for instructing the youth of the nation and for governing colleges and universities, reliable information about faculty members' activities, attitudes, and values is surprisingly limited. Relatively few empirical studies of faculty have been conducted. Of the studies that have been made, only a few have obtained data directly from faculty members themselves, and only a handful have included more than one institution.

Two major themes dominate the study reported here—the centrality of teaching in the lives of faculty, and faculty support for certain kinds of teaching practices and educational change. The data on which the study is based were obtained directly from faculty members of a variety of kinds of institutions of higher education. Attention was focused on learning how faculty members feel about a number of sometimes controversial and always important aspects of the role of a college teacher, and a particular effort was made to examine the range and diversity of faculty members in higher education, to determine the characteristics of different types of faculty, and to consider the implications of this diversity for educational policy and practice. More specifically, the study was designed to address several important questions concerning teaching.

- How important is teaching in the lives of faculty members? Does the academic reward structure make adequate provision for effectiveness in teaching, or is research emphasized at the expense of teaching?
- What are some alternative ways to conceive of teaching, and in what institutional settings is each appropriate?
- How many faculty members extend their teaching beyond the classroom? How do they convey their accessibility to students, and what benefits do they derive from out-of-class interaction?
- What do faculty members think about current efforts to increase the proportion of interdisciplinary courses, to give academic credit for work on community projects, and to change admission requirements in order to accept more students from minority groups?
- Given the academic specializations of faculty members, what prospect is there for the success of interdisciplinary programs?
- What kinds of faculty members favor and/or oppose efforts by students to obtain a larger voice in the governance of colleges and universities?
- How can answers to these questions be used to improve the quality of teaching and learning?

To address these questions, we conducted a survey of faculty members of several colleges and universities during the winter of 1968–69. A Faculty Characteristics Questionnaire was developed which contained a wide range of items concerning faculty opinions, beliefs, perceptions, activities, satisfactions, and biographical information. Our sample of faculty members was selected from six colleges and universities located in three states. The six schools do not constitute a large enough sample to be representative of all colleges and universities, but it was felt they might provide a large number of faculty members representative of the range and diversity found in American higher education. Since faculty members—not institutions—are the primary focus of this study, the schools were selected to assure that different kinds of college professors could be studied. The schools are described briefly below as they were *at the time of this study.*

The University of California, Davis. The Davis campus, one of nine in the statewide university system, is located in a small community about 20 miles from Sacramento. From its founding in 1909 until the late 1940s, it was predominantly a school of agriculture. The opening of a college of letters and sciences in 1951 and the subsequent addition of a wide range of graduate programs and schools of law, engineering, and medicine have progressively transformed it from a single-purpose school into a comprehensive university. Like other campuses of the University of California, its major purposes include providing undergraduate education, offering graduate and professional education through the doctoral level, and conducting original research. At the time of our survey, 700 faculty members were employed, and the school enrolled 10,200 students, all but a few of them full-time. The undergraduate students, as required by state law, came from the top 12.5 percent of high school graduating classes.

California State College at Los Angeles.* This school was founded in 1947 in response to lobbying of World War II veterans who wanted a public institution where students graduating from the two-year Los Angeles City College could work toward bachelor's degrees. During its first ten years, it was located on the site of the city college, and it was jointly administered by the City of Los Angeles and the State of California. Since it opened its new campus in 1958, it has grown rapidly and had 22,300 students and 1050 faculty members when this study was conducted. Freshmen and sophomores made up only about 15 percent of the student body, and in this commuter school 57 percent of its enrollment was composed of part-time students. The campus is one of several in the California State University and College system that have been charged with providing both undergraduate and graduate education through the master's level. Admission of undergraduates is on a first-come-first-served basis for those students who are among the top 25 percent of high school graduates.

Chabot College. Located in the San Francisco Bay area, Chabot College opened in 1961 as the first campus of a multicampus district that serves the needs of six associated public school systems. Like most public community colleges, it maintains two different kinds of educational programs; it provides the first two years of liberal arts or

---

* Since this survey was conducted, the California State Colleges have become the California State University and Colleges. Nevertheless, they remain one of the three public segments of California higher education and continue to have the same general functions. We have continued to use the "state college" label for what is actually now, California State University, Los Angeles.

preprofessional programs for those students who will seek higher degrees at other institutions, and it maintains a vocational-technical program in such areas as library technology, dental hygiene, automotive mechanics, and traffic management. In addition, there is an adult education program for local residents. An open admissions policy, found throughout the community colleges in California, provides that any student who graduates from high school or reaches the age of 18 will be admitted. The college had a total of 330 faculty members, 179 of whom were full-time teachers; all of them possessed the required state certificates for community college teaching. The college enrolled 9500 students, most of whom were part-time.

Hofstra University. Founded in 1935 in Hempstead, Long Island, a short drive from New York City, the university until a few years ago served a commuting student body with undergraduate and master's level programs. At the time of our study, the university was involved in an aggressive development program designed to transform the school from a predominantly undergraduate college into a comprehensive university. It had already started two Ph.D. programs and planned several more; it had acquired land and had started to extend its physical plant; and it had built two dormitories. Since 1964 the university has maintained a small experimental college with a separate academic program devoted largely to the general education of undergraduates. In 1968–69 these programs were staffed by 450 faculty members who instructed 12,000 students, about half of whom were part-time.

Bard College. Located in the Hudson River Valley in upstate New York, Bard College was founded in 1860 as a denominational school, and it remained little changed until after World War I. At that time, a development program was instituted and the school became affiliated with a major university. As a result, the school took on an experimental image and made many changes which it has maintained. The college has since gained its independence from both its church and university affiliations. A favorable faculty–student ratio, small size, and dormitory living provide a community atmosphere dedicated to the kind of intellectual endeavor typical of some of the selective liberal arts colleges in the Northeast. The college enrolled 600 students and had a faculty of 60 at the time of our survey.

The University of Puget Sound. Founded in 1888 by a local church conference in Tacoma, Washington, the university is still dedicated to providing its students with "a balance of educational, cultural, social, and religious activity . . . within a Christian framework." The church ties are more than formal, since at the time of the study graduation requirements included three semester hours of religious study. Primarily an undergraduate school, the university expected its 3800 students, drawn primarily from the immediate area, to live either at home or in school dormitories. There were 225 faculty members.

Our sample of faculty members consisted of the entire full-time faculty at Chabot, Hofstra, Bard, and Puget Sound and a random selection of 400 each from the Davis and Los Angeles campuses. A total of 1556 questionnaires were distributed; 1085 were completed and returned; and 1069 were received in time to be included in the analysis. The overall response rate was 70 percent, and the institutional response rates varied from 79 percent at Puget Sound to 53 percent at Bard. (A summary of the relevant information about the number of questionnaires distributed and returned and the response rates for each institution is contained in Appendix I.)

About two weeks before the questionnaire was mailed, we sent a preliminary letter to each faculty member in the sample and included a brochure describing the Center for Research and Development in Higher Education at Berkeley as well as a brief description of the purposes and procedures of our study. About a month after the questionnaire was distributed, each nonrespondent was sent a short follow-up letter with an enclosed postcard asking him to check whether he had returned the questionnaire already, whether he was completing it, or if he had misplaced it and needed another.

Our procedure produced a sample of faculty members that closely resembled the national population in a number of demographic variables. The proportion of faculty members of each sex, in junior and senior ranks, with and without doctoral degrees, and in each of the major divisions of study closely approximated the proportions contained in two much larger national surveys by Trow and Lipset (Bayer, 1970) and by Dunham, Wright, and Chandler (1966)—surveys designed to study the entire faculty population. We believe that our sample contains approximately the same range of diversity among faculty members as exists in the whole of American higher education. (The comparative data for the three studies are contained in Appendix I.)

In reporting findings from this study, in most cases simple percentages were chosen as the most widely used and understood mode of data presentation. While levels of statistical significance were generally omitted in the tables and text, the differences discussed are all statistically significant at the .05 level of probability and in most instances at the .01 level. In several of the analyses, the respondents were divided as nearly as possible into thirds on one of the faculty variables of key interest, and the relationships of other variables to these measures were examined with the use of chi-square and Kruskal-Wallis tests.

Study I of this book reports the main results of this survey, and it is organized around the twin themes of teaching and educational change. The importance of teaching in the lives of faculty members is discussed in Chapter 2. Included in our analysis are data concerning the satisfaction faculty members take from teaching, the role of teaching in the advancement system, and faculty attitudes toward teaching evaluation. Although faculty members are generally committed to teaching, the ways in which they go about their teaching vary widely. Two alternative teaching styles and their contexts are discussed in Chapter 3.

Some faculty members make special efforts to extend their teaching beyond the classroom and to hold discussions with students about their future education and career goals, and about intellectual and campus issues. Chapter 4 analyzes out-of-class student–faculty interaction from the faculty point of view, evaluating the amount and kinds of interaction, the ways certain faculty members make themselves accessible to students, and the benefits they derive from this interaction.

Faculty attitudes about a variety of educational changes are discussed in Chapter 5. Particular emphasis is given to determining the educational philosophies, teaching practices, and attitudes toward students that characterize those faculty members who tend to favor or to oppose educational change in general. Two specific kinds of changes are dealt with in Chapters 6 and 7. The faculty cultures that form around the academic disciplines are analyzed and the implications they hold for interdisciplinary study are presented in Chapter 6, while Chapter 7 is concerned with faculty attitudes toward student participation in making both academic and social policies.

Chapter 8 discusses the need for both policy and operational support for the improvement of teaching. Some examples are included of administrative supports, legislative actions, and supports from disciplinary and professional associations that are directed toward improving undergraduate teaching.

Chapter 2

The Importance of Teaching

To what extent are college professors committed to teaching? How important do they feel teaching should be in pay and promotion decisions? How do they feel about procedures for evaluating teaching?

Most of the faculty members in our survey consider teaching a central activity as well as a major source of personal satisfaction. Despite the widespread feeling that most college and university faculty teach only as a way of subsidizing their scholarly research, when we asked them to indicate major sources of satisfaction in their lives, the most frequent answer was, "teaching." That answer was given by 88 percent of our respondents, while 61 percent of them indicated that they derive a similar degree of satisfaction from "scholarly activity."

Since most faculty members at most institutions spend much of their time teaching, and since they have chosen to become and to remain college teachers, it is not surprising that researchers (McGee, 1971; Sanford, 1971) have found that teaching is a source of great satisfaction. And even though a majority of the faculty members in our own study indicated an interest in scholarly activity and an involvement in other nonteaching activities such as public service affairs, campus governance, and private consulting, the teaching role remains central in their lives. Some observers maintain, in fact, that many of these nonteaching activities can and do serve to enhance the quality of teaching by broadening the experiences and expanding the competencies of professors (Parsons & Platt, 1968).

A large part of the recent controversy about the importance of teaching has to do with the reward structure, especially with the criteria used in making decisions about promotions and salary levels. One subject of discussion in this controversy centers on the importance that should be attached to these criteria; for example, whether teaching effectiveness should be given more or less importance than research productivity.

Faculty members in our survey were asked to indicate how much importance they believed should be given to certain criteria—"effectiveness as a teacher," "research and scholarly activity," "school service," "community service," and "seniority"—in the making of decisions pertaining to promotion and salary matters. Table 1 presents their responses. Teaching effectiveness received the largest number of responses, with 92 percent of the total indicating that they felt it should be of high importance. Research and scholarly activity were considered to be of high importance to 63 percent, while school service, community service, and seniority were felt to be of high importance by much smaller percentages of the faculty members responding.

The high value placed on teaching effectiveness is underscored by the fact that an overwhelming majority of respondents at five of the six institutions believed that it should be given the highest importance. Only at the state university was it maintained that research ought to be held equal in importance with teaching—a reflection, perhaps, of the "publish or perish" requirements of universities. The important point is, however, that in most other institutions of higher

Table 1 Faculty Views of the Importance that Should Be Attached to Certain Criteria in Making Decisions Pertaining to Promotion and Salary Matters, in percentages

Criteria	Not Important and Somewhat Important	Moderately Important	Quite Important and Very Important
Effectiveness as a teacher	2	6	92
Research and scholarly activity	11	26	63
School service	32	41	27
Community service	51	28	21
Seniority	61	25	14

education, faculty members spend the bulk of their time in teaching activities, and believe that teaching effectiveness should be the cornerstone of the reward structure.

But there are, obviously, some differences between what criteria faculty members believe *ought to* apply in determining promotion and salary policies and what they may believe *actually does* apply. The faculty members in our survey were also asked to indicate how much importance they feel each of the several criteria is given in actual pay and promotion decisions at their schools. Table 2 presents their responses to this question. Only 39 percent of the respondents believed that teaching effectiveness was of high importance in actual practice, and almost as many—34 percent—believed that it was of very little importance or of no importance at all. Although there were institutional differences in the type of nonteaching activities that faculty indicated were emphasized in their colleges' existing reward structure, at every one of the schools in the survey, even at the smaller colleges where the importance of good teaching is presumably emphasized, faculty members replied that they think teaching effectiveness should be given far more weight in pay and promotion decisions than it actually is.

This wide discrepancy between the desired and the actual suggests widespread faculty dissatisfaction with the lack of emphasis placed on the value of teaching in the incentive system. A large number of faculty appear to have concluded that good teaching is probably not the most promising means to advancement in their institutions. This perception of the reward structure may have serious negative implications for the quality of teaching on American campuses.

Table 2   Faculty Views of the Importance Actually Attached to Certain Criteria in Making Decisions Pertaining to Promotion and Salary Matters, in percentages

Criteria	Not Important and Somewhat Important	Moderately Important	Quite Important and Very Important
Effectiveness as a teacher	34	27	39
Research and scholarly activity	27	20	53
School service	27	32	41
Community service	66	23	11
Seniority	38	20	42

But if teaching is not as important a means to advancement as faculty indicate it ought to be, what activities are rewarded instead? Is research the golden road to promotion? A further reading of Table 2 might suggest as much: More than half of the respondents—53 percent—reported that they believe research is given highest importance. However, an analysis of responses by institution produced mixed results. At the state university campus scholarly activity was seen as the primary vehicle of advancement, but at each of the five other schools research productivity was believed to be given even less value than teaching. The analysis by institution, in fact, revealed that faculty members at the five schools thought that research, as well as teaching, was underemphasized. Only the state university faculty believed that research was given as much importance as it should be given in promotion and salary decisions.

At schools that lack explicit research missions, faculty dissatisfaction with the degree of importance attached to research is probably understandable. The responses to two items elsewhere in the questionnaire indicate that most faculty members in the survey believe teaching and research are mutually reinforcing. The vast majority agreed that involvement in research makes for more exciting teaching and that teachers involved in research are more likely to keep up to date in their fields. In short, they believe that research improves teaching and that it consequently should be more highly prized. About a quarter of the faculty members, however, acknowledged that tension does sometimes exist between research and teaching; they agreed with the notion that research takes up time that might otherwise be given to preparation for teaching or to activities with students.

A substantial proportion of faculty members seemed to feel that advancement is rather strongly influenced by school service and seniority. Yet only a small number of these faculty members expressed belief that these criteria *should* be important to decisions affecting advancement. It is obvious that these faculty members feel that merit, particularly meritorious achievement in teaching and scholarly research, rather than seniority, should be the basic consideration of the advancement system.

The role that such extrinsic motivational factors as salary and promotion play in the improvement of teaching is sometimes questioned. It has been asserted that the good teacher is—or ought to be—motivated by his own intrinsic desire to teach, rather than by the lure of money or rank. The survey data show, in fact, that the vast majority of faculty members do derive intrinsic gratification from their teaching. But intrinsic and extrinsic satisfactions are closely related. A promotion or salary increase may give a faculty member the self-confidence that comes from being well-regarded by his colleagues, while failure to receive an extrinsic reward may make him question his own competence. Even committed and effective teachers may suffer a diminution of their efforts if they are denied recognition for their achievements.

Closely associated with the reward structure is the issue of teaching evaluation. If teaching effectiveness is to be rewarded, there necessarily must be some procedure by which it can be appraised. But the nature of the procedure, as it varies from campus to campus, has been the source of some controversy. There are questions about whether information should be obtained in a formal, systematic manner, or whether the all-too-usual technique of gathering hearsay evidence is preferable, and about the appropriate roles of deans, department chairmen, teaching colleagues, and students in the procedure. The faculty members in our survey were asked their views on these questions.

A surprisingly large majority—72 percent—of the respondents said that they believed their schools should have formal procedures for evaluating teaching effectiveness. Such a large response reflects, perhaps, frustration with the informal systems that traditionally have been used. Undoubtedly, too, some of these faculty had in mind their own preferred evaluation procedures, which are not, of course, reflected in the questionnaire. But the response is significant because it shows that a very large proportion of faculty members willingly accepts the principle of teaching evaluation.

Those favoring formal procedures were also asked who they thought should be involved in such procedures, and the replies are equally informative. Students were named by 82 percent of the respondents, teaching colleagues by 76 percent, department chairmen by 74 percent, college deans by 36 percent, and alumni by 23 percent. It is apparent that faculty members prefer to give those persons most closely involved with their teaching the largest say in evaluating it. Students, teaching colleagues, and department chairmen are likely viewed as friendly critics; surely they have the greatest knowledge about the teaching practices of most instructors.

The value of students as judges of teaching effectiveness was examined by another item. Only a slight majority of the faculty members—52 percent—agreed with the statement, "students are the best judges of how effectively their professors teach." No doubt a less extreme statement—for example, that students can make important contributions to any formal procedure for the assessment of teaching—might have found greater agreement. The significant point is that more than half of the respondents even agreed with the extreme statement. Similarly, massive national surveys (Bayer, 1970; Bayer, 1973) have discovered favorable faculty attitudes toward student evaluation of teaching. For example, in the 1973 survey of 42, 000 faculty Bayer found that 69 percent agreed with the statement "Faculty promotions should be based in part on formal student evaluations of their teachers."

One of the primary reasons why faculty members are favorably disposed toward the principle of teaching evaluation, as well as student involvement in it, is evident from responses given to another item in the questionnaire. Each faculty member was asked to indicate how he thought most students would regard him as a teacher. Interestingly, only eight teachers, out of the 1069 in the total sample, reported that they would be regarded as below average. Eight percent believed that they would be rated about average; 22 percent indicated slightly above average; 50 percent said well above average; and 19 percent claimed that they would be rated among the very best. It is obvious that many faculty members hold highly favorable, and possibly exaggerated views of their own teaching prowess, and they most likely think that they should be rewarded for it.

Of course, not only do teachers tend to rate their teaching above average, students also tend to rate it high (Hildebrand, Wilson, & Dienst, 1971). Procedures that provide teachers with feedback about the ways students perceive their teaching behavior hold promise for improving both their self-perceptions and their teaching styles (Centra, 1972 b).

These findings suggest several courses of action that may be taken to improve the quality of teaching. The most important course of action would be for institutions to devise and maintain policies and procedures that would assure that faculty members could advance themselves by pursuing teaching excellence. Procedures to assess and reward teaching are being followed in growing numbers of institutions.

In hundreds of schools students have taken the initiative and have already set up their own evaluation procedures. Faculties at some of these schools have supported formal student evaluation on the ground that an assessment, if it is to be done at all, had better be done well—(meaning, in all probability, with faculty assistance). A national survey of changes in colleges and universities (Hodgkinson, 1970) revealed that 38 percent of the institutions investigated reported increases in faculty willingness to accept student course evaluations. For the many schools that have not yet done so, the time is ripe to initiate formal evaluation programs which include student participation.

Much has already been learned about student ratings of teaching (Sockloff, 1973; Costin, Greenough, & Menges, 1971). As teachers become more familiar with this information, they will hopefully feel less threatened by student assessment. Experience is increasingly demonstrating that student evaluation of teaching is both valuable and practicable. The number of objective instruments available is growing. Some recent examples include instruments developed by Hildebrand, Wilson, and Dienst (1971), by McKeachie (1969), and by Centra (1972a), and alternative procedures have been set forth by Eble (1970).

An even greater impact on teaching has been made by student involvement in the operation of the reward structure. At some schools students have demanded and been given membership in appropriate faculty advancement committees. The mere fact of their physical presence at meetings of such committees sometimes seems to have increased the importance other committee members attach to teaching criteria, since faculty members find it difficult to minimize the importance of teaching in front of students. Too, student members of these committees are more likely to advocate that primary importance be given to a candidate's teaching effectiveness. Considering that most faculty members have reservations about giving students major roles in setting academic policy in general (see Chapter 7), it is understandable that students have so far been given only token membership in most such committees.

Aside from the matter of student participation, there are other ways that institutions can give greater visibility to their commitment to good teaching. One way is individualization of faculty contracts, sometimes called "growth contracts," wherein the weight teaching will carry in each advancement decision can be specified. Individualized contracts can be negotiated to suit special needs, and they can designate the exact proportions of time that any professor will spend in his various activities. The institution can then obtain what it most needs to operate its programs, and the professor can accommodate his present stage of personal and professional development. To illustrate: One professor might contract to spend half of his time teaching an introductory course and the other half advising students; another might contract to spend three-fourths of his time on a research project and one-fourth teaching an advanced course in a related subject; and still another professor might contract to devote half of his time to committee work and the other half to teaching. Individualized contracts, carefully devised, can ensure that the needs of both individual faculty members and their institutions can be met.

Not only do individualized contracts allow for specific faculty assignment, but they also provide an explicit basis for individual evaluation. A faculty member can be assured that he will be evaluated on what he has explicitly agreed to do, rather than on vague and general criteria. His teaching will be evaluated as teaching, and his research will be evaluated as research. He will know precisely what is being evaluated, and he will know how much it counts toward his own advancement.

Our research has shown that, contrary to the beliefs of some critics of contemporary higher education, professors are concerned about the quality of teaching. They are dissatisfied with the frequent disregard for good teaching in criteria for advancement, and they are sympathetic to formal teaching evaluation procedures that include student judgments. They have confirmed their commitment to teaching. This commitment has already been put to good use by colleges and universities that have developed new procedures for the assessment of teaching and for the rewarding of teaching effectiveness with salary increases and promotions. Such procedures, if adopted and followed with skill and compassion, can reinforce the intrinsic gratifications faculty members derive from teaching. Perhaps they can also be used to further increase faculty members' commitments to teaching and to the improvement of teaching.*

* A more extended analysis of the sociopsychological environment of college teachers, along with suggestions for improving the context for teaching, can be found in J. G. Gaff, & R. C. Wilson. The teaching environment, *AAUP BULLETIN*, 1971, **57**, 475–493.

Chapter 3

Alternative Styles of Classroom Teaching

Over the last several decades a considerable body of research has been developed on teaching and the evaluation of its effectiveness (Travers, 1973; Gage, 1963; Ryans, 1960). Although most of the literature on teaching concentrates on the primary and secondary levels, there has been increasing attention given to college teaching. Much of it has focussed on the study of teaching methods and the evaluation of teachers with relatively little consideration of the diverse contexts in which college and university teaching occurs, the differing goals among both teachers and students, or the variety of philosophical orientations toward education found at different institutions.

A study of teaching at a large California university, conducted by Hildebrand, Wilson, and Dienst (1971), identified several types of effective teaching and concluded that there is no single model of effectiveness. Some evidence was also presented that suggested that teachers who exhibit different teaching styles appeal to students who have different college goals. Consequently, there is good reason to believe that it is important, in exploring the dynamics of college teaching and defining its effectiveness, to examine alternate models. Teaching effectiveness must be considered in relation to specific desired educational goals and the different learning styles of students.

It is widely recognized that institutions differ in their instructional, research, and service functions, as well as in composition of their faculties and student bodies. But the teaching–learning process is often assumed to be essentially the same at every school. Two teaching models are investigated in this chapter in order to better understand how teaching practices reflect faculty conceptions of their educational missions and the characteristics and motivations of the students they teach.

Three of the schools included in our survey—the state university campus, the state college, and the community college—are located in California. They represent three types of higher education institutions which have been assigned distinct educational functions, as delineated in the Master Plan for Higher Education adopted by the California legislature (Donohoe Higher Education Act, 1960). The University of California campuses were authorized to conduct original research and to provide graduate instruction through the doctoral level, as well as undergraduate instruction. The California State College campuses were empowered to concentrate on undergraduate education, to offer graduate instruction only at the master's degree level, and to conduct only that research which was consistent with the instructional program. Community colleges were charged with providing both transfer liberal arts education and terminal vocational-technical education at the lower division level. With minor exceptions, the state university was allowed to admit only those undergraduates who were in the upper 12.5 percent of their high school graduating classes; the state colleges could enroll undergraduates from the upper 25 percent; community colleges were expected to accept any student who had graduated from high school or had reached the age of 18. These three distinct missions, specifying levels of student ability—along with associated differences in faculty assignments, salaries, work loads, and state financial support—had the effect of transforming the educational system into a hierarchy.

Although the California Master Plan said nothing about the nature or style of teaching to be provided at each type of institution, only equality of instruction could assure equality of educational opportunity as envisioned by the plan and also allow for transfers between levels. Yet, the kind of instruction offered by any school in the system was bound to be heavily influenced by the position of that school within the hierarchy. We expected, therefore, that one of the latent consequences of the Master Plan would be a differentiation of goals and teaching practices among the faculty in the three types of institutions.

A comparison of faculty goals and classroom practices in the three schools did indeed reveal a number of such differences. Taken together these data suggest that differences among the student bodies of the three types of institutions as prescribed by the Master

Plan are paralleled by differences in the kinds of faculty and in the kinds of teaching and learning practices characteristic of those institutions.

Among the most noticeable of these differences are faculty views concerning educational goals for undergraduates. Respondents from the three schools were asked which of several goals they favored; their responses are presented in Table 1. The goal most frequently chosen was a broad general education, but sizable numbers of faculty also indicated goals of self-knowledge and personal identity, knowledge and skills directly applicable to careers, and understanding and mastery of some specialized body of knowledge.

It is apparent from Table 1, however, that the order of goal preference varies widely from one kind of institution to another. For example, at the community college a larger percentage of faculty members favored the goal of self-knowledge than at the state university, while a smaller percentage preferred the goals of skills and knowledge mastery. Furthermore, the implications of these different educational goals can be observed in teaching behavior. Certain instructional approaches are more common at the state university, while other approaches are more common at the community college. The state college employs a mixture of the two.

Table 1   Primary and Secondary Goals of an Undergraduate Education as Viewed by Faculty Members, in percentages[a]

Goals	Community College	State College	State University
Knowledge and skills directly applicable to student careers	31	37	37
Understanding and mastery of some specialized body of knowledge	13	24	31
Preparation for further formal education	22	17	14
Self-knowledge and personal identity	53	33	30
Broad general education	56	59	61
Knowledge of and interest in community and world problems	20	22	21

[a] Percentages are based on both first and second goal preferences, so the total for each school equals 200 percent (e.g., 31 percent of the community college faculty members indicated "Knowledge and skills directly applicable to student careers" as a primary *or* a secondary goal of an undergraduate education).

Table 2   Teaching Practices and Attitudes of Faculty, in percentages[a]

Teaching Practices and Attitudes	Community College (N = 138)	State University (N = 303)
Subject-matter approach:		
Lecture to class	6	33
Use detailed notes	28	38
Student-centered approach:		
Favor individualized assignments	52	37
Encourage students to pursue own interests	42	31
Favor judging student performance in relation to capacities	58	34
Control and structure:		
Feel class attendance should be optional	21	47
Give unannounced tests	26	13
Take precautions to prevent cheating	44	19
Describe objectives	51	35
Follow textbook closely	63	41
Intrinsic (student) motivation:		
Basic interest in subject	44	64
Are challenged intellectually	28	41
Extrinsic (teacher) motivation:		
Communicate own enthusiasm	77	56
Make courses relevant	49	21

[a] Percentage is the percentage of faculty members in each institution who scored in the upper third of the total distribution for each item ... except for the four motivation variables, where percentage is the percentage of faculty members indicating each of those variables.

At the university, faculty more commonly adopt a teaching method that involves lectures and detailed notes, presumably because they believe it the most effective way to convey the basic facts of their subject matter to large numbers of students. In fact, the characteristic instructional method of university faculty members is a *subject-matter approach.*

By contrast, as shown in Table 2, community college faculty members are distinguished by their somewhat more *student-centered approach.* For example, the community college faculty members are more willing to individualize their teaching. A large proportion of them agreed that class assignments should be individually tailored to the needs and interests of each student and that students should be encouraged to pursue their own individual interests in courses. Obviously, allowing students to go their separate ways means little if they are held to a single standard of achievement at the end of the course, so it is of particular interest that these faculty members also affirmed that the classroom performance of a student should be judged in relation to his capacities. On this matter, university faculty members differed markedly; far more of them insisted that students should be evaluated against absolute standards of achievement. And this view is clearly in keeping with their greater emphasis on the educational goal of mastering a body of knowledge.

These and other responses suggest that teaching behavior may very well reflect the perceived characteristics of the students being taught. The academic motivation of students may be expected to shape the kinds of teaching strategies adopted by faculty members. For example, faculty members were asked to indicate which factors motivate most students to learn in the courses they teach: the university faculty members more often said that the students have a basic interest in the subject matter and that they are challenged intellectually. The community college faculty, by contrast, saw themselves in a situation where they must motivate students to learn. The technique of the university lecture, the mere presentation and analysis of subject matter, would not be sufficient for the community college instructors, more of whom said that they attempt to generate and "communicate enthusiasm for the subject matter" and that they try to "make the courses relevant to the lives of students." Undoubtedly the preference for self-knowledge goals leads these community college faculty members to adopt teaching methods that elicit greater student participation and involvement than is possible with the lecture method. And they probably feel a need to involve students in classroom activities in order to engender an interest in the subject matter.

It might be expected that teachers who are subject-matter-oriented would be less willing to grant freedom to students than those teachers who are more student-oriented. Our survey findings suggest that this is not necessarily so, however. More of the university faculty thought that class attendance should be optional, and fewer said that they give unannounced tests and quizzes in order to check up on their students. University students are presumably more academically able than community college students—as specified by the Master Plan—and probably have more intrinsic interest in ideas. Consequently, university faculty can more easily adopt a laissez-faire approach, especially when they evaluate student achievement against uniform standards at the end of the term.

On the other hand, community college faculty are more concerned with controlling the behavior of their students. Not only do fewer of them feel that class attendance should be optional, but more of them give unannounced tests to assure that students actually do their work, and they are far more likely to "take precautions to prevent cheating in examinations." They also more frequently report that they "describe objectives at the beginning of each class session" and that they "follow the textbook closely." These practices seem to reflect a belief that community college students need guidance in their learning process. The community college faculty, precisely because they are concerned about the development of their students, attempt to exert benevolent control over them. Such a disposition toward control and discipline may be, at least for some of these faculty members, a carry-over from high school teaching practices; Medsker (1960) has found that many community college faculty have moved up from the ranks of secondary school teachers in an effort to improve their professional status. But these faculty members are also more likely to call students by their first names, probably again because the practice is in keeping with their efforts to create student–teacher relationships that can be instrumental in helping students to get involved and to learn.

Since community college faculty members appear to work harder to motivate their students, they may be expected to show a more favorable attitude toward pedagogy. This inference is supported by the data. More of these teachers agreed that "prospective college faculty should receive training in teaching skills as part of their graduate education," and more of them thought that modern technological aids—such as the use of media and computer-based instruction—"hold promise for improving college teaching." Because they believe that the teacher plays an active role in affecting student learning, they also reported a belief that if a student fails a course it is usually at least partly the fault of the teacher. University faculty members, on the other hand, showed the least interest in pedagogy of the three faculty groups, most likely because they believe that knowledge of the subject area is the most important ingredient in teaching ability. The matter was summed up by one university faculty member who commented: "We try to hire the best authority on the subject, and he is by definition the best teacher of the subject."

Two fairly coherent configurations of teaching have emerged from this analysis. Teaching at the university is more characteristically subject-matter oriented. The purpose is to help students acquire certain specialized knowledge and skills, and it is pursued by means of lectures and classes that feature intellectual analysis and discussion. It is assumed that university students are interested in ideas, and the faculty attempt to interest them by making courses intellectually challenging. Although university faculty adopt a laissez-faire attitude toward students, they expect students to meet absolute standards of achievement, which are set by the teacher. Relationships with students in class are task-oriented, sometimes to the point of appearing impersonal, but collegial relationships with certain students are also established outside of class. Pedagogy is held in low esteem.

By contrast, the teaching configuration found among community college faculty is more student-centered. More of these teachers emphasize self-knowledge and the personal development of students, and they attempt to achieve this goal by encouraging somewhat more student participation in classroom activities. Since community college students are less expected to evidence intrinsic interest in ideas, teachers employ a variety of strategies to motivate them; they attempt to communicate enthusiasm, to make courses relevant, and give as much guidance to the learning process as possible. These faculty are more attuned to the individual differences among students, and more of them are willing to allow students to pursue their own interests, and to evaluate student achievements in relation to their abilities. Because these faculty face important pedagogical challenges in their own teaching, they display a favorable attitude toward efforts to teach teachers how to teach.

Teaching at the state college cannot be adequately characterized as either subject-matter-oriented or student-centered. On almost all questionnaire items concerning teaching practices, the percentages of responses of faculty members at the state college fell between those of the other two types of schools. Yet these responses do not seem to comprise a genuine alternative approach; the approach contains elements of the other two approaches. It has been suggested by other research (Dunham, 1969; Harcleroad, Sagen, & Molen, 1969) that state colleges have not developed a unified purpose or role. This may be because the state college draws faculty from a more diverse pool than do either the university or community college. The university recruits faculty who have a strong orientation to scholarship and research, since their survival in the system depends highly on their scholarly productivity. The community college, because it has no formal charge to produce new knowledge, recruits faculty whose task is clearly defined as teaching. The state college tends to draw faculty of both types. Many of their faculty are really university oriented and wish to maintain themselves as subject-matter specialists and researchers. Many of them are more like community college teachers who have little interest in research and are more student-centered in their teaching.

Some evidence of the frustrated upward aspiration of many of these state college faculty can be found in the fact that they see deficiencies in their students. In their responses to questionnaire items about student deficiencies, 61 percent said that their students "lack involvement with ideas and intellectual concerns," while 40 percent said the students "lack mastery of the content of college courses." The university faculty are relatively more satisfied with their students, probably because the students are actually less deficient in these ways, and the community college faculty are more satisfied because they do not hold high expectations for their students in these areas. But the state college faculty seem to have higher aspirations (a larger proportion of them than community college faculty hold skills and mastery goals and a smaller proportion hold self-knowledge goals) while believing that their students are not particularly interested in ideas (fewer of them said their students were interested in academic matters). This conflict, institutionalized in the California Master Plan, is a major source of dissatisfaction among many faculty members at the state colleges. The conflict may also explain why teaching practices at the state college occupy an intermediary position between the subject-matter approach at the university and the student-centered approach at the community college.

In general, then, the primary goals of institutions affect the teaching practices found at those institutions. But it may also be seen that there are, within these institutions, individual differences in both teaching objectives and practices. Although the student-centered approach is dominant at the community college, for example, there remain certain community college faculty members who do not subscribe to this view of educational purpose and method. As Table 1 has shown, 56 percent of the community college faculty saw a broad general education as among the two most important goals for undergraduates, and 53 percent saw self-knowledge and personal identity as among the two most important goals. But 31 percent also embraced the goal of knowledge and skills directly applicable to student careers. Several questions must be asked, then: Do the instructors with different goals behave in the classroom as their colleagues do? Or are their teaching practices more akin to those of the university faculty members who share their subject mastery objectives? To what extent do institutional norms affect the teaching styles adopted by individual faculty members whose purposes differ from a substantial proportion of their colleagues?

To obtain answers to these questions, further analysis was made of the data obtained from the three kinds of schools. Analysis of the data from the state university and the community college provides significant information.

In order to obtain mutually exclusive groups, subsamples of the faculty members at each institution were divided into two groups according to their goal preferences. The first group included those faculty members who accepted, as either the most, or second most important goal, "knowledge and skills directly applicable to student careers" and "understanding and mastery of some specialized body of knowledge," but who *did not* subscribe to the goal of "self-knowledge and personal identity." The second group included those faculty members who subscribed to "self-knowledge and personal identity" as one of the two most important goals, but who *did not* subscribe to the goals having to do with skills and mastery. Table 3 presents the results of this grouping, along with the relationship between the groups and certain teaching practices.

A careful review of Table 3 indicates that the manner in which preferred individual educational goals relate to teaching practices is considerably modified by the teaching norms that characterize the different institutions. The operation of institutional press is not universal, however, and in some instances results indicate that complex interaction effects may be present. But for the most part, faculty members at each institution, even though holding different goal orientations than their colleagues, were found to share similar teaching styles to a greater extent than those who shared similar goals but taught at distinctly different schools.

To illustrate: community college faculty members who subscribe to goals of skills and mastery adopt certain teaching practices less often than faculty members subscribing to these goals at the university; they are less inclined to lecture to their classes, use detailed notes, or think class attendance should be optional. Community college faculty members in this group more often indicate that they "follow the textbook closely," "take precautions to prevent cheating," "think class assignments should be individually tailored," "give unannounced tests," "feel that student performances should be evaluated in relation to capacities," "communicate their own enthusiasm," and "strive to make their courses relevant to the lives of students." All of these practices and beliefs demonstrate that these community college faculty, in spite of the skills and mastery goals they subscribe to, share the student-centered approach of their teaching colleagues. In their teaching behavior they clearly adhere to the characteristic teaching

Table 3 Teaching Practices Related to Educational Goals, in percentages[a]

Teaching Practices and Attitudes	Skills and Mastery Groups		Self-Knowledge Groups	
	Community College (N = 41)	University (N = 136)	Community College (N = 54)	University (N = 55)
Subject-matter approach:				
Lecture to class	2	37	7	27
Use detailed notes	39	52	21	33
Student-centered approach:				
Favor individualized assignments	46	33	63	44
Encourage students to pursue own interests	27	25	54	40
Favor judging student performance in relation to capacities	49	23	62	51
Control and structure:				
Feel class attendance should be optional	10	46	28	51
Give unannounced tests	29	19	15	7
Take precautions to prevent cheating	56	23	42	15
Describe objectives	56	36	46	36
Follow textbook closely	73	45	60	31
Intrinsic (student) motivation:				
Basic interest in subject	63	63	39	51
Are challenged intellectually	29	44	28	42
Extrinsic (teacher) motivation:				
Communicate own enthusiasm	83	53	70	56
Make courses relevant	46	20	56	36

[a] Percentage is the percentage of faculty members in each institution who scored in the upper third of the distribution for each item . . . except for the four motivation variables, where percentage is the percentage of faculty members indicating each of those variables.

style of their institution. They may share educational goals with certain university faculty members, but their attempts to reach these goals are modified by the practices of their more immediate colleagues in the community college.

033977

Faculty members who subscribe to the self-knowledge goal, but not skills and mastery goals, also show different teaching styles depending upon the kind of institution. The university faculty members subscribing to this goal, for example, remain subject-matter-oriented in their teaching, well within the range of the predominant and characteristic style at the university. They adopt, more often than subscribers to this goal at the community college, lecturing to their classes. They are more apt to believe that students are challenged intellectually, and, despite their student-oriented goals, they are less inclined to make individual class assignments, encourage students to pursue their own interests, evaluate student performance in relation to capacities, and attempt to make the course relevant to students' lives.

While these findings support the notion of institutional press, they do not suggest that individual goals have no effect on teaching practices. Although in most instances teaching styles within institutions are similar despite goal differences, the findings also indicate that educational goals do affect teaching behavior to some extent. Community college faculty members in the skills and mastery group appear to be a bit more subject-matter-oriented than is typical of their school colleagues, and the university faculty members in the self-knowledge group appear to be a bit more student-oriented than the university faculty members on the whole. Consequently, it should not be assumed that the teaching styles that characterize an institution are necessarily models strictly adhered to by all faculty members within the institution. There is diversity within institutions, and some individual differences can be attributed to disagreements concerning the goals deemed important in undergraduate education.

SUMMARY AND IMPLICATIONS

The alternative teaching styles presented here may be characteristic of institutions that vary on the continuum from student-centered to subject-matter-oriented. Regardless of a school's position along this continuum, certain teaching practices follow from the faculty member's educational purposes. For many schools, the educational mission may be less clearly defined than in the examples presented here, but the examples should offer some insight into the relationship between teaching goals and practices.

One of the most important determinants of teaching practices seems to be the ability level of students. While students may not have

membership in faculty committees that determine institutional goals or teaching practices, it is clear that their own personal and intellectual characteristics play an important role in shaping the teaching styles of faculty members.

Linked to the characteristics of the students is the institutional mission. An essential aspect of the community college is its commitment to students of a wide range of ability, and this commitment requires that faculty members modify their teaching practices in order to guide students through the learning process. With such a strong commitment to serve students, there is greater pressure to accomodate student needs. The university commitment, on the other hand, is directed more toward knowledge than toward students. The students are expected to be highly dedicated to obtaining knowledge, and they cannot succeed in the system if they fail to meet the standards defined by the faculty. The student, in short, is expected to adjust to faculty standards; indeed, he is required to meet these standards. Intellectual quality is placed above student needs.

Since faculty members move from one institution to another, especially during their early teaching years, they may believe themselves equally prepared to accept and carry out the objectives of different types of institutions. Faculty seldom accept appointments with full knowledge of the educational goals and teaching practices of the institutions that they join. As a consequence, individual dissatisfaction among faculty members may stem from conflicts between individual teaching styles and normative environmental pressures, although this conflict is rarely articulated or understood.

Both the subject-matter approach found at the university and the student-centered approach found at the community college has its own kind of excellence and its own kind of failing. Faculty members who must help students achieve a sense of personal identity may require different kinds of institutional supports, such as opportunities for closer and more extended interaction with students, than those who must help students master a body of knowledge. Efforts to improve instruction in these different kinds of schools will require strategies that take cognizance of the kinds of teaching and educational objectives which are to be practiced and valued.

Chapter 4

Accessibility and Interaction with Students

At the core of most critiques of American higher education is the assertion that effective education requires close working relationships between faculty and students. Indeed, whether implicitly or explicitly, many recent indictments of higher education have been made from a philosophical vantage point that posits the importance of close faculty–student interaction. This interaction is seen not only as a means by which the transmission of knowledge and student intellectual growth is best facilitated, but as an educational goal in and of itself. If these critics are right, of equal importance to faculty teaching styles and practices within the classroom may well be the formal and informal teaching activities that take place outside the classroom.

Most of the research that has been conducted in this area suggests that in most institutions out-of-class interaction is fairly infrequent and superficial (Feldman & Newcomb, 1969). In a study of Columbia University undergraduates, for example, Thielens (1966) found that less than half of the students had visited at least three instructors to talk about their studies, one or more times during the school year. Only 11 percent of the freshmen students in this study knew one or more of their instructors on a personal basis, and by the time the students were seniors only 55 percent of them had developed such a relationship.

There is an assumption in much of the literature on the subject that students greatly desire close contact with faculty. The percentages of students who express such a desire, however, have been found to vary considerably with the settings in which they are studied and with the kinds of students involved—from 17 percent on some campuses to 65 percent on others (Feldman & Newcomb, 1969, pp. 249–50, where the major results of most studies of the subject to that date are cited). And in Chapter 14 of this book, evidence is cited that student expectations about relationships with faculty have not been met in reality. Nearly half of entering freshmen in eight institutions had expressed the belief that getting to know faculty would be personally satisfying, but when these students became seniors the number who felt that faculty–student relationships had been important to them dropped significantly. At the same time, however, the students as seniors had not given up a view held as freshmen that an ideal college is a close-knit community in which there is a chance to know both students and faculty.

Most research on faculty–student interaction is based on data obtained from students, but there also exist a few studies that report faculty experience in this area. Gamson (1967), for example, found at a small cluster college that faculty estimates of the proportion of students they saw on a regular basis ranged from about five to 25 percent. And in a study of 22 departments in a major university, Vreeland and Bidwell (1966) found wide variation in the frequency of faculty–student interaction.

The present analysis attempts to go beyond previous studies in several ways. It includes faculty from six highly diverse institutions instead of only one institution; it investigates the relationship between the total amount of interaction outside of class and a number of faculty characteristics to see if there are, in fact, certain faculty characteristics that seem to facilitate or impede interaction; and it explores some of the possible consequences of out-of-class interaction that may have implications for the improvement of college teaching. This last exploration seems particularly important. Although nearly everyone feels that faculty–student interaction is desirable, and although many institutions are making concerted efforts to increase faculty–student contact (with the creation of cluster colleges, mini-colleges, and similar projects), little is known about the actual benefits that can be expected to accrue to either faculty or students from increased interaction beyond the classroom.

FREQUENCY OF INTERACTION: METHOD

The measure used for determining frequency of interaction was faculty members' response to this item on the questionnaire:

> Faculty members have a variety of contacts with students outside the classroom. Please try to estimate how many times during the past two weeks you have met with students* in the following capacities. Count only conversations of 10–15 minutes or more.

In the questionnaire six role capacities were defined in terms of the content area of conversations or discussions with students. They are:

Instuctor. To discuss intellectual or academic matters with a student.

Educational advisor. To give a student basic information and advice about his academic program.

Career advisor. To help a student consider matters related to his future career.

Friend. To socialize informally with a student.

Counselor. To help a student resolve a disturbing personal problem.

Campus citizen. To discuss a campus issue or problem with a student.

Response alternatives for the number of meetings in each of the six discussion categories (role capacities) were: none; one or two; three or four; and five or more.

As an indicator of overall frequency of interaction, the frequencies reported for the six discussion categories were summed, and the faculty members were then divided into three groups according to the total number of out-of-class interactions reported with students during the two-week period. The groups were: high interactors (25 percent of the faculty members); medium interactors (31 percent of the faculty members); and low interactors (44 percent of the faculty members).

The same groups were also used as the bases of subsequent analyses exploring faculty characteristics that might be expected to facilitate or impede a faculty member's out-of-class interaction with

---

* A cover letter and the wording of other items in the questionnaire emphasized that the focus of the study was on undergraduate students.

students. These faculty characteristics were of two types. First, there were those characteristics that were expected to act as facilitators or impediments primarily because they tended to affect the amount of time a faculty member had available for interacting with undergraduates beyond the classroom. These were factors that located the faculty member's position within the academic profession and its division of labor, such as academic rank, membership and participation in professional associations, publishing productivity, and the amount of time a faculty member devoted to research, administration, and the teaching of graduate students.

Second, there were those characteristics that were expected to act as facilitators or impediments primarily because they reflected a faculty member's social and psychological accessibility for interacting with students. These characteristics were termed social-psychological factors because they were aspects of the individual's psychological proclivities and his interpersonal style. To determine the effect of these factors three teaching style scales were used, as well as several scales that measured the faculty member's attitudes toward students and the educative process that might be expected to communicate to students a faculty member's openness—his willingness and desire for interaction with students beyond the classroom.

AMOUNT AND TYPE OF INTERACTION

Of the six discussion categories for which faculty members were asked to report number of meetings, the two that showed the greatest number of contacts were, not surprisingly, those most central to the professional purposes of a college or university professor—to discuss intellectual or academic matters with a student (the role of instructor) and to give a student basic information and advice about his academic program (the role of educational advisor). As Table 1 indicates, 95 percent of the faculty members reported at least one student interaction in the capacity of instructor, and 40 percent reported five or more such encounters; 92 percent reported at least one instance of giving educational advice, and 45 percent reported five or more such discussions.

Of these two types of discussions, the one most frequently reported—having to do with intellectual or academic matters—might be expected to occur most often as a natural extension of instruction given in the classroom. The fact that 60 percent of all faculty respondents reported fewer than five such discussions (10 minutes or

Table 1   Frequency of Out-of-Class Interaction with Students in Six Role Capacities, in percentages

Role Capacities	Number of Discussions of 10 Minutes or More with Students during Two-Week Period				
	None	1–2	3–4	5 or More	Total[a]
Instructor	5	24	31	40	100
Educational Advisor	7	21	26	45	99
Career Advisor	19	45	21	15	100
Friend	26	34	22	18	100
Counselor	46	41	9	5	101
Campus Citizen	48	38	10	4	100

[a] Total percentages vary because all percentages were rounded to nearest whole numbers.

more) in a two-week period may underscore for some critics the relative infrequency of out-of-class interactions between most faculty members and their students. If the two-week period covered by this question is typical, then it may be estimated that in a 15-week semester 60 percent of the faculty had fewer than 37 out-of-class interactions with students in this single capacity alone. Assuming that most faculty members are responsible for teaching more than 37 students each term, this rate suggests that the majority do not even see each of their students once during a term to discuss intellectual or course-related matters. It should be noted, too, that the faculty members in this study may well be reporting meetings with the same students on repeated occasions; from the simple number of interactions reported for each discussion category (role capacity), it cannot be determined whether the numbers reflect frequent discussions with the same students or less frequent interactions with different students. In the subsequent study (Study II), which was based on student as well as faculty data, however, it was found that only a small proportion of students seek frequent interaction with faculty; the majority of students reported little contact with faculty beyond the classroom.

In the present study, faculty members reported decreasing amounts of contact with students in the role capacities of career advisor, friend, counselor, and campus citizen—as also indicated in Table 1. These roles may be viewed as optional types of interaction with students, and they probably are not as frequently expected by students as the instructor or educational advisor roles. But the fact that they are optional may also explain why they are more strongly related to the faculty characteristics that seem to facilitate or impede out-of-class interaction.

FACULTY CHARACTERISTICS AND INTERACTION WITH STUDENTS

Faculty characteristics found to be significantly related to out-of-class interaction consist of attitudes and behaviors central to teaching and learning as an interactive process; they are *not* the variables that locate the position of the faculty member within the academic profession generally. Thus, none of the factors expected to act as barriers to interaction—because they compete for time, interest, and energy with the task of teaching undergraduates—were found to be significantly related to interaction in this study. Specifically, the amount of out-of-class interaction that a faculty member reported was not found to be affected by academic rank, membership and participation in professional associations, or productivity in publication of articles, books, or monographs. Even the percentages of time faculty members reported spending in activities that are expected to detract directly from time available to undergraduates—such as time devoted to research, administration, and the teaching of graduate students—were not significantly different for faculty members who reported different amounts of contact with students beyond the classroom.

The characteristics found to be associated with the total amount of out-of-class contact a faculty member has with students were those we have termed social-psychological. They include faculty beliefs or attitudes that support a view of education as an interactive process as well as faculty behaviors that appear to invite discussion both within and beyond the classroom. Faculty attitudinal support for interaction was measured by a scale of *Personalization of Faculty–Student Interaction*; some defining terms of this scale are "Informal out-of-class contacts with faculty members are an important part of a student's education" and "Students learn class material best if a teacher takes a personal interest in them." Endorsement of the ideology expressed in this scale was found to be positively related to contact with students outside the classroom. Table 2 presents the results of measurement by this scale.

In addition to a belief in the value of out-of-class interaction, sheer physical availability of faculty members may be expected to influence

Table 2   Social-Psychological Accessibility and Frequency of Out-of-Class Interaction with Students, in percentages

Personalization of Faculty–Student Interaction Scale	Frequency of Interaction		
	High	Medium	Low
High	45	34	23
Medium	28	28	22
Low	28	37	54
Total[a]	101%	99%	99%

[a] Total percentages vary because all percentages were rounded to nearest whole numbers.

the amount of interaction. Since most out-of-class contacts probably occur in faculty offices, one logical indicator of availability is the extent to which a faculty member keeps office hours. While 70 percent of all respondents reported that they always keep office hours, and while another 21 percent said that they often do, there were significant differences in reporting by the high-, medium-, and low-contact groups. Of the high-contact faculty group, 78 percent said that they always kept office hours, whereas 65 percent of the low-contact group said they were as consistently available.

These findings suggest that the amount of contact a given professor has with his students is a function of his belief in the value of relating to them on a personal, one-to-one basis. Keeping regular office hours is one way he has of letting students know that he is available for out-of-class contact. It is probably only a necessary—not sufficient—condition for interaction, however. A teacher may be available to students without being truly accessible to them—in the sense of being willing and even eager to listen, to exchange ideas, and to help if he can. Accessibility goes beyond physical availability. The data seem to suggest, in fact, that the importance that a faculty member attaches to personal interaction with students is, more probably, an important component of his social-psychological accessibility.

IN-CLASS TEACHING BEHAVIORS AS CUES TO ACCESSIBILITY

In order to stimulate interaction with students, a teacher's accessibility—as evidenced by his attitudes, values, and beliefs—must be communicated, however subtly, to his students. This communication no doubt occurs in a variety of ways and in a variety of settings, including direct invitations in the classroom for the student to meet the teacher outside the classroom. But there are also in-class behaviors that may serve to provide students with cues to the teacher's social-psychological accessibility.

Three teaching practices scales were used in this study to measure in-class teaching behaviors. The three scales are:

Classroom Participation Practices. The highest loading item of this scale is "invite students to help make class plans or policy." This scale also includes such practices as asking for student evaluation of a course and encouraging student participation in classroom discussions.

Discursive Practices. The highest loading item of this scale is "discuss points of view other than my own." The scale also includes such other practices as relating work to other fields of study and encouraging discussions of issues that go beyond class reading.

Evaluation Practices. The highest loading items of this scale showed a preference for giving essay exams instead of objective exams, for using term papers, and for grading without the use of a curve.

All three scales were positively related to amount of interaction with students, as Table 3 indicates.

These results are consistent with the general hypothesis that in-class teaching behaviors may be taken by students as cues to a professor's accessibility for out-of-class discussions. Teachers who interact the most frequently with students outside the classroom show a greater willingness to solicit the views of students in class (*Classroom Participation Practices*), to discuss a variety of points of view (*Discursive Practices*), and to allow students to express their ideas through essay exams and term paper assignments (*Evaluation Practices*).

It would appear that faculty members who frequently interact with their students more often manifest their accessibility for contact in a variety of ways. But even more striking is the converse finding: faculty members who have little interaction with their students outside the classroom manifest their inaccessibility for such contact by a variety of subtle cues, which say to the student, in effect, that the process of learning is essentially a process of fulfilling formal classwork assignments and mastering the prescribed content of a given body of knowledge. When each of these teaching styles, rather than frequency of interaction, is treated as the prior or independent variable,

Table 3   Classroom Teaching Practices and Frequency of Interaction with Students Beyond the Classroom, in percentages

Frequency of Interaction	Classroom Teaching Practices		
	Classroom Participation Scale Score		
	High	Medium	Low
High	36	25	16
Medium	32	38	25
Low	32	38	59
	—	—	—
Total	100	101	100
	Discursive Practices Scale Score		
	High	Medium	Low
High	37	26	16
Medium	30	33	31
Low	32	42	53
	—	—	—
Total	99	101	100
	Evaluation Practices Scale Score		
	High	Medium	Low
High	31	26	20
Medium	35	30	31
Low	35	44	49
	—	—	—
Total	101	100	100

it is apparent that faculty members who have little contact with students do little to invite such contact; indeed, they may do much to discourage it. Of the 351 faculty members who scored among the bottom third in the *Classroom Participation Practices* scale, most had little or no out-of-class contact with students in any capacity, and very few interacted to much extent with students beyond the classroom. Comparable differences in frequency of interaction were found for faculty members scoring low on the other two teaching practices scales and on the attitudinal scale *Personalization of Faculty–Student Interaction.*

Thus it would appear that in the teaching styles of these low-interacting faculty members there is significantly less encouragement of expression, controversy, or the active participation of students in their own education. There is the suggestion, as well, that the interactive style characteristic of these faculty members in their classrooms tends to discourage the exchange of ideas beyond the classroom.

On the other hand, a faculty member who encourages his students to participate in the conduct of courses communicates to them that he is interested in what they think and is open to engaging in intellectual exchange or discussion with them. A faculty member who relates his course content to other fields of study and to current social problems, as well as to the history of ideas, communicates to his students a wider range of interests and his feeling that these topics are relevant and worthy of being developed further by discussion and synthesis. A faculty member who uses the essay or nonobjective approach in evaluating what students have learned communicates to his students his belief in the open-ended, unfinished nature of knowledge, and he thereby invites greater discussion, and even controversy, about the correctness or truth of any given answer to a given question.

SOCIAL-PSYCHOLOGICAL ACCESSIBILITY AND TYPES OF INTERACTION

The hypothesis that out-of-class interaction is a function of social-psychological accessibility requires further elaboration when the relationship between teaching styles and frequency of interaction in each of the six individual role capacities is explored. In the two most frequently reported role capacities, instructor and educational advisor, for example, no significant relationship was found between the number of out-of-class interactions with students and the faculty attitudes and behaviors that reflect accessibility for interaction. Students seeking counsel about their academic programs or about issues, ideas, or assignments in a specific course are generally not free to choose among faculty. Ordinarily an educational advisor is assigned to a student early in his studies, and the teacher of a given course—except in the case of independent study—is determined, at most institutions, by the faculty and administration, rather than by the student.

Actually, there is little freedom of choice in these two roles for either faculty or students. Both roles are, to a large extent, mandatory or prescribed for faculty. Faculty members are expected—indeed, in some instances required—to see students to answer questions about course assignments and projects or to periodically advise a student who has been assigned to him for that purpose. And the student has little freedom of choice in selecting faculty members to seek out for these kinds of discussions once a faculty member has been chosen or assigned and once he is enrolled in a course.

The other four faculty role capacities—career advisor, friend, counselor, and campus citizen—offer much more freedom of choice. Few faculty members are specifically required to act in these roles vis-a-vis their students. A teacher, if called upon by a student to play any of these roles, is generally free to play the role or to beg ignorance, disinterest, or incompetency in the area, referring the student elsewhere or otherwise avoiding further discussion. The student is also perfectly free to choose from among all of the faculty known to him, either personally or by reputation, the one teacher who he feels would be most open and/or knowledgeable about the subject he wishes to discuss; he is not limited in his choices of faculty as he is when he seeks advice about a course or a program of studies. It is logical, then, that factors of social-psychological accessibility play a significant role in faculty–student discussions in optional areas and that they have little effect on interactions that are fixed or prescribed.

POSSIBLE CONSEQUENCES OF OUT-OF-CLASS INTERACTION

It is generally presumed that faculty–student interactions have value for students. The rewards of interaction, however, like the process itself, are not unidirectional—teachers may also benefit from contact with students. The data indicate that faculty members who have more contact with students are also more likely to be very satisfied with the stimulation they receive from students (see Table 4). And since there were no significant differences between the faculty groups concerning the satisfaction they derive from colleague stimulation, this response to students is probably not just an instance of a general tendency to be gregarious. The difference is specific to their interaction with students. Judging from an analysis of their teaching styles, it seems likely that high-interacting faculty members do in fact receive more stimulation from students; certainly they more often encourage interaction. As indicated in Table 4, high-contact faculty members are also more likely to feel that students would rank them as among the very best of teachers, and they more often include teaching among the major satisfactions in their lives. In short, these faculty members appear to take pride in their work and to derive greater intrinsic enjoyment from their teaching than their colleagues do.

Table 4 Consequences of Interaction and Frequency of Out-of-Class Interaction with Students, in percentages

Consequences of Interaction	Frequency of Interaction		
	High	Medium	Low
Satisfaction with stimulation received from students: Very satisfied	36	19	11
Belief that most students would rank him "among the very best" teachers on his campus	24	22	14
Teaching said to be a major satisfaction in his life	93	90	85
Responded "don't know" the adequacy of student's preparation in three or more of eleven skill and knowledge areas at their institution	19	23	32

Out-of-class interaction also increases the knowledge faculty members have about their students' strengths and weaknesses, their interests, problems, and perspectives. While low-contact faculty members, for example, were more likely to say that students graduating from their colleges lack mastery of content of college courses, they were also significantly more likely to claim that they do not know whether their graduates are adequately prepared in such diverse areas as reading, writing, creative thinking, and breadth of knowledge.* These skills and types of knowledge, taken together, form a central part of a liberal arts education. And since information about student inadequacies in these areas is requisite to curriculum planning and change, to teaching and learning evaluations, and to academic counseling—activities in which faculty members participate to a great extent—it would seem worthy to note that out-of-class interaction with students is an important source of such knowledge.

High-contact faculty tend to hold favorable views of their graduates' capabilities and achievements in these skills and knowledge areas, but there are some other important areas in which they are more likely than low-contact faculty members to feel that students are deficient. They are more likely to say that students

* It should not be thought that faculty ignorance of these matters is a function of disciplinary area; there were no significant differences in the amount of contact with students reported by faculty in the humanities, social sciences, natural sciences, or applied fields.

graduating from their colleges show a lack of concern with political, social, and economic issues, that they display an uncritical acceptance of the values of society, and that they are overconcerned with security.

In the absence of data on the students themselves, this information is important for what it says about the faculty members who hold these views. High-contact faculty members are civic-minded—in the classical sense of being involved—and they are concerned with the affairs of society as a whole. The data reveal that they are significantly more likely to include among the major satisfactions in their lives such interests as participation as a citizen in community affairs and participation in activities directed toward national or international betterment. It may be, then, that in comparison with themselves, their students do seem less concerned, less involved, less critical, and more complacent about the status quo of society and the body politic.

Related to this picture of high-contact faculty members as a less complacent and more involved group in society is the fact that they are also less likely to favor the status quo in higher education. They are not only more likely to favor changes within their institutions, but they are also more likely to favor changes in a direction compatible with their own teaching behaviors, their styles of interaction, and their attitudes toward students. A majority of these faculty members desire an increase in the amount of faculty–student interaction, in the number of interdisciplinary courses, in the use of independent study, in the proportion of courses directed at social problems, and in the extent to which students help determine the content of course. Low-contact faculty members, by contrast, prefer to leave these practices unchanged or even to decrease them. (Chapter 5 presents a fuller analysis of the correlates of attitudes toward educational change.)

SUMMARY

These data suggest that there is a fairly coherent set of attitudes and practices which constitute a kind of social-psychological accessibility to out-of-class interaction with students. Faculty members who interact most frequently with students value such interaction the most. They also more often manifest their accessibility in the way they go about teaching their courses. Their relations with students, both inside and outside the classroom, are qualitatively and quantitatively different from those of their colleagues. They encourage and experience a broader range of discussions with students than is ordinarily prescribed for the role of a college teacher. And it appears that faculty members who are accessible to students manage to interact with some frequency outside the classroom despite competing responsibilities in research, administration, and graduate training. Conversely, faculty members who make themselves psychologically inaccessible to students fail to have much contact with students whether or not they experience competing demands on their time and energies.

Faculty members who have the most interaction with students beyond the classroom also seem to reap personal and educational benefits from such interaction. Out-of-class interaction seems to enhance both the enjoyment and the sense of accomplishment a faculty member can derive from teaching, and it seems to increase his knowledge of students' academic strengths and weaknesses in areas central to a college education.

Even more dramatic evidence of the consequences of out-of-class interaction for both faculty and students is reported in Study II (Chapter 14). One aspect of those findings tends to validate the findings presented here: faculty members who report the most frequent interaction with students in the six discussion areas (role capacities) have also received the greatest number of nominations from their colleagues as outstanding teachers and as teachers who have significant impact on the lives of students. They have also received the greatest number of nominations from college seniors as teachers who offer the most stimulating courses and who have contributed most to the students' personal and/or educational development. It is surely of major significance that acknowledgement should be made by colleagues and by students themselves of the effectiveness and impact of those faculty members who most frequently engage in interaction with students beyond the classroom. Since this out-of-class interaction with students is considered by faculty and students to be an important component of teaching effectiveness, it ought to be more heavily weighted in evaluation and in the reward structure of colleges and universities.

Chapter 5

Attitudes
toward Change

The discussion so far has dealt with aspects of teaching as it is practiced within the context of traditional colleges and universities. But new developments in higher education, already underway, suggest that new teaching practices will be required from many faculty members and that new faculty–student relationships will be needed. These new developments include the creation of experimental programs and colleges, the increase in off-campus learning and work experiences, and the acceptance by educational institutions of social groups not previously represented to a large extent in higher education.

Not much is yet known about how faculty members regard these new developments or other proposals for educational change. Anecdotal evidence is mixed: in some instances faculty members have been criticized for embracing uncritically certain changes such as including affective components in their teaching, while in other instances faculty members have failed to support significant proposals for change. The research picture is equally cloudy: two recent surveys (Martin, 1969; Lipset & Ladd, 1971) present evidence that many faculty members hold favorable attitudes toward certain kinds of change. In both cases, however, the investigators have also offered their beliefs that, on balance, faculty members are not strong supporters of academic reform—especially reforms that would affect their own teaching practices. Faculty tend to be more liberal and willing to embrace changes in society than changes within the university. Thus the subject is ripe for closer examination.

Two basic questions may be asked: How do faculty members view a sampling of recent educational changes, such as the creation of courses dealing with contemporary social problems, independent study programs, and student involvement in community action projects? And what are the characteristics—educational goals, teaching styles, relationships with students, related attitudes, and positions in the academic system—of those faculty members who generally favor or oppose these kinds of educational change?

Our findings about faculty attitudes toward certain selected educational changes are presented in Table 1. The majority of faculty

Table 1 Faculty Attitudes Toward Selected Educational Changes, in percentages

Educational Change	Increased	Left the Same	Decreased
Proportion of students from minority groups	78	22	1
Amount of informal interaction between faculty and students	71	28	1
Proportion of interdisciplinary courses	68	28	4
Use of independent study	67	31	2
Proportion of courses directed at contemporary social problems	59	37	4
Extent to which students help to determine the content of courses	40	54	6

	Agree Strongly	Agree Somewhat	Disagree Somewhat	Disagree Strongly
Students should be allowed to earn academic credit by working in community projects directly related to their academic interests	39	43	11	7
Colleges should lower their formal admission requirements in order to accept more students from minority groups	15	37	26	22

members surveyed favored educational changes that increase the proportion of students from minority groups, the amount of informal interaction between faculty and students, the proportion of interdisciplinary courses, the use of independent study, and the proportion of courses directed at contemporary social problems. A majority also favored allowing students credit for work in community projects and lowering admission requirements for minority students.

Although these issues do not encompass the most radical of recent proposals for revamping higher education, they do represent responses to the broad issues of social relevance and student voice. Taken together, they probably reflect a trend in education toward making colleges more socially active and responsive to the needs of students and of society.

Faculty members, needless to say, favored some of these changes more than others. They were most sympathetic to increasing the proportion of students from minority groups (but less so if it meant lowering admissions standards to achieve that purpose), and they were most opposed to increasing the extent to which students should help to determine course content.

SUPPORTERS AND OPPOSERS

Just as there is variation among faculty members in the degree of support they would give to any specific changes, so too there is variation among them in their general willingness to support changes at all. Since the success of efforts aimed at academic reform depends in large measure on identifying allies and opponents, it is important to understand the characteristics of both the faculty members who support change and those who oppose it. One part of our research has been an attempt to identify these characteristics.

In order to construct a measure of general attitude toward change, eight questionnaire items were combined into an index of change orientation (*Current Issues in Educational Change*). Each faculty member was given a score on this scale, and the entire sample was divided into high-, middle-, and low-scoring groups. High- and low-scoring groups were then compared, and they were found to differ from each other in a number of important ways.

Of fundamental significance is the fact that these groups differ in their conceptions of the purposes of an undergraduate education. The group favoring these kinds of changes tended to endorse self-development as the most important goal of education, while the group opposing such changes tended to favor the development of vocational and technical competence. The goal of self-knowledge and a sense of personal identity was chosen by 35 percent of the high-scoring group and by only 13 percent of the low-scoring group. Alternative goals concerned with preparation for a career and mastery of a specialized body of knowledge were chosen by 38 percent of the low-scoring group and by only 15 percent of the high-scoring group.

The group most in favor of these changes, in keeping with its preference for self-development goals of education, felt that teachers should be more actively concerned with providing a personalized atmosphere to encourage the personal development of students. They scored higher than the change-resistant group on a scale composed of such items as "the emotional and personal development of a student should be as important to a teacher as his intellectual development" and "students learn class material best if a teacher takes a personal interest in them." The change-resistant group more often rejected personalization of the educative process.

While most faculty members hold rather permissive attitudes toward the regulation of students' personal lives, those who are most favorable to change are far more permissive. When a scale composed of items concerning the necessity for college rules about personal behavior (such as the use of alcohol, women's dormitory hours, premarital cohabitation, the use of marijuana, and similar issues) was trichotomized, 52 percent of the group favoring change were in the most permissive category, rejecting the necessity for regulation of the personal lives of students. Only 12 percent of the group opposed to change were in this category. This view of the faculty members who favor change is consistent with the philosophy that the self-development of students is best facilitated by allowing them freedom to make decisions about their personal lives and to learn from the consequences. Those opposed to change apparently believe that few students are capable of using these freedoms responsibly.

The group opposed to change tended to hold a no-nonsense approach to teaching, and to value the fundamentals. They expressed greater agreement on such questionnaire items as "students too often want to speculate on important issues before they master the relevant basic facts" and "without test and grades to prod them, most students would learn little." The group favoring change tended to express greater faith in the academic motivation of students, a view consonant with their confidence in the ability of students to benefit from the absence of externally imposed social rules and regulations.

Because students have maintained that one of the changes needed in higher education is the more active participation of students in the governance of their colleges, questions were asked of faculty members about the role students should play in determining academic and social policies. Responses show that change-oriented faculty members are far more inclined to have students participate in both the academic and nonacademic governance of their schools than are the faculty members who oppose change. Both groups, however, appear more conservative about student participation in academic policymaking than in policymaking concerned with students' social lives. (These issues are discussed further in Chapter 7.)

The three scales concerned with classroom teaching practices were also used in the analyses. Faculty members who favor educational change scored significantly higher on the scale called *Discursive Practices* and the *Classroom Participation Practices* scale. On the *Evaluation Practices* scale, the change-oriented faculty members more often supported less structured procedures, such as essay exams and term papers, while the faculty members opposing change favored more structured procedures, such as objective exams and grading on a curve.

Since not all teaching takes place in the classroom, the attention faculty members give to students outside of class was also investigated. It was found that faculty members who favor certain educational changes have significantly more out-of-class interaction with students than those opposed to change.

The educational values, attitudes, and teaching practices of change-oriented faculty are clearly thematically related to the types of changes they advocate. They believe in self-development goals for undergraduate education, student freedom to regulate personal behavior, and more active student participation in campus governance, and they have more confidence in the ability of students to benefit from self-directed learning. They are more discursive and student-centered in their classrooms, as well as in out-of-class interaction with students, and they are eager to see colleges become more responsive to social issues and to the needs of minority groups and the community at large. They see a need for more relevant and intellectually integrative approaches to teaching and learning. Their academic areas are most likely to be the humanities and the social sciences.

Faculty members who oppose the current trends toward academic change, on the other hand, are more likely to want students to acquire vocational and technical competence, to de-emphasize the need for close faculty–student relationships, to hold more restrictive views about student personal life, to have a theory of teaching and learning that emphasizes the importance of external motivations, and to deny students a significant role in either academic or social policy-making. In their teaching they are more likely to emphasize factual understanding, to be instructor- or subject-matter-oriented, to employ structured evaluation procedures, and to have little contact with students outside of class. They are disproportionately found in the academic areas of the natural sciences and many fields of applied study.

These profiles of faculty members who favor or oppose academic change are similar to the profiles of alternative teaching styles discussed in Chapter 3. Given the student-centered teaching approach adopted at the community college in our survey, faculty members there may be expected to give greater support for the kinds of changes studied here. And given the subject-matter approach found at the state university campus in our survey, faculty members there may be expected to hold less charitable attitudes toward these changes.

Perhaps the most important finding regarding the two groups has to do with the power to make policy. An analysis of the rank and sex of the respondents, for example, revealed that significantly more of the change-oriented faculty members came from the lower academic ranks and that women were overrepresented in the group. The group opposing change, on the other hand, was composed disproportionately of men in the senior academic ranks. These status differences indicate that those most opposed to change may hold the greatest policymaking power within their institutions, a fact that doubtless tends to restrain the forces for change.

In order to complete these profiles and perhaps make them more useful, it is important to point out some variables that did not differentiate faculty members who favor or oppose change. The groups did not differ regarding the number of books published or papers read at professional meetings, the number of national professional associations to which they belong, the number of national professional association meetings attended within the last three years, the percentage indicating scholarly pursuits as a major source of satisfaction in their lives, or the relative importance attached to research and scholarly activity in promotion and salary decisions.

But a word of caution is in order concerning the interpretation of these profiles. The kinds of changes that have been discussed here are historically conditioned. They are the kinds of changes that have been advocated most vocally by political and educational radicals on college campuses since the outbreak of the Berkeley Free Speech Movement in 1964 and, more recently, by commissions on academic reform. They include a call for social action, curricular relevance, and student participation. The present era of change is markedly different from earlier ones. In the post-Sputnik era of the late 1950s, for example, would-be reformers tried to divert American higher education from its previous focus on liberal arts and the development of culturally sophisticated men and women and make it focus more earnestly on advancing the scientific and technological capabilities of the nation by developing scientific and technological specialists. Those proposed changes may well have been favored by a different breed of academics than those who, in the current era, support changes that would place the university at the center of social action and that call for humanizing higher education.

The profiles of faculty members who favor or oppose academic change may be expected to vary, depending on the general nature of the changes being proposed. Indeed, the more academically conservative faculty members described in this study may well be the very ones who were most change-oriented in the 1950s, who demanded an upgrading of standards, increased specialization, and a greater emphasis in the natural science and technological fields. Having achieved their ends in large measure, these faculty members may now have become well entrenched in the college power-elite, comfortable with the status quo, and opposed to the new humanists and the changes they champion.

MOVING THE FACULTY

Evidence from this survey reveals that there is a large reservoir of faculty sentiment in favor of several changes in educational practices. The main problem for would-be educational reformers, therefore, evidently does not lie in convincing faculty members of the need for the types of changes studied here, but in mobilizing existing sentiment.

This formulation poses at least two critical questions: If faculty members are favorable to current trends in educational reform, why are they so widely regarded as being opposed to this type of innovation? And how can their attitudes be translated into action to effect change?

The view that faculty members are intransigent and opposed to change no doubt reflects the fact that actual change has come ever so slowly in higher education, and probably also reflects a lack of knowledge about faculty attitudes toward innovation. But the greatest pressure and sympathy for reform lie, as already noted, with faculty members primarily from the lower academic ranks who, because of their exclusion from key academic policymaking committees, may be nearly as disenfranchised as the students they support. Their location in the humanities and the social sciences also suggests that these faculty members may have less power in bringing research monies and prestige to their institutions, further reducing their influence in determining both the direction of and the necessity for educational reform.

The barriers to reform resulting from the structure of academic governance have been noted by other writers (Eckert, 1970; McConnell & Mortimer, 1971). Academic senates and their committees are at best cumbersome structures that make it difficult for a faculty to act on even the most trivial proposal. Research at one university (Mortimer, 1970) indicated that the faculty senate was controlled by an oligarchy composed of persons who held high rank and who had been at the school for a longer period and had compiled a longer publication record than the average faculty member on the campus. The power exercised by this conservative oligarchy (which the present findings suggest would be more likely to oppose change) was a major reason why recommendations for significant change emanating from three special committees of the academic senate during the preceding five years went largely unheeded.

Another factor that may impede change is disagreement among faculty members about how to achieve it. Faculty members who favor increasing the proportion of interdisciplinary courses, for instance, are not always also willing to give up some courses in their own departments. Or on another issue: Data from this survey show that while more than three-fourths of the faculty members said that the proportion of minority students should be increased, only about half of them were willing to alter existing admissions requirements to accommodate these students. Even when faculty members are agreed on objectives, their lack of a consensus about the means to those objectives may immobilize them. In keeping with their training as rational and critical scholars, faculty members may question a good idea to death—not out of malice nor opposition, but simply out of habit.

Although faculty members are generally well trained in their academic disciplines, most of them are not trained to be college teachers. The natural result of this lack of preparation for teaching is that faculty members tend to be ignorant about educational change options and about alternative teaching roles. Martin (1969) has reported evidence that faculty members are not informed about new developments that have important implications for teaching and learning. This finding was further substantiated by Gaff and Wilson (1971), who called for the creation of in-service training programs to inform faculty members about innovative approaches in education, the results of research concerning various aspects of higher education, and alternative faculty roles. Currently faculty development programs and teaching improvement centers are being established by increasing numbers of institutions, including all types of colleges and universities. Such programs hold much promise for expanding faculty awareness of what is possible and thus for effecting change.

In recent years faculty members have been faced with such amounts of new knowledge that they are hard put simply to keep abreast of developments in their own fields of specialization. They are expected to conduct and publish original research, consult with government and industry, participate in professional associations, and contribute to their local communities. Consequently, few of them may feel they can afford the time or emotional investment required for conceptualizing and executing substantive educational change— unless they are given released time. Some schools have provided professors such released time, have paid them to work on proposals during the summer months, or have permitted them to offer "planning courses" as part of their regular work load. In the last analysis, it seems that educational change cannot be brought about until some faculty members are given time, however arranged by their institutions, to analyze the needs that are not being met by current resources, to develop well-conceived proposals to meet those needs, and to guide the plans through the labyrinth of academic governance.

Factors such as the power and status of faculty members who oppose change, the cumbersome nature of academic governance, the disagreements over means, the ignorance of faculty members about change options, the economics of support for program planners, and time for faculty members to devote to putting sentiment into action are serious obstacles to educational reform. All of them help to explain why, despite the fact that individual faculty members generally favor reform, college faculties as a whole appear to be opponents of change.

Strategies devised at certain schools, however, have been successful in overcoming many of these barriers. One increasingly common device is the organization of alternative programs on a single campus. This organizational form may bring together several change-oriented faculty members and students within a semiautonomous structure and, at the same time, permit faculty members who hold more traditional views to continue using their methods in other portions of the same campus. An institution differentiated in this way may be both innovative and traditional, thereby appealing to both types of faculty members. Such a campus may be better able to meet the variety of needs of both teachers and students than is possible in an undifferentiated school.

It is not necessary to have the unanimous support of a faculty in order to effect change. Indeed, unanimous opinions are rare, and they are often suspect among academics. Innovators, instead of lamenting the fact that faculty members resist change, might better work with those who wish to promote change and try to bolster that group with like-minded students and administrators—for there is considerable diversity within these groups, too. Innovators can often effect significant changes by crossing formal status lines and drawing support where it is available.

Another technique for obtaining faculty support for innovation utilizes faculty members who are highly respected by their colleagues. St. Olaf College, for example, establishd in 1969 an experimental college staffed with six faculty members, five of whom were drawn from the existing faculty, had long experience with the college, and enjoyed reputations as good teachers. During the first year, a survey of faculty attitudes toward the new college revealed a high degree of support, and more support, curiously, was found among the senior faculty than among the junior faculty. In view of the strong negative feelings engendered by cluster colleges in similar settings, it is important to note that this endorsement of the new college by the established faculty can be traced in large measure to the fact that familiar and respected colleagues led the venture.

While these strategies may help to bring about specific changes, they may not necessarily produce something that is possibly more important—continuous renewal of an institution. The data showing that junior faculty members are more favorable to change than their senior colleagues imply that one way to promote continuous change is to devise mechanisms by which younger faculty members can have a high degree of influence on school and departmental policies. In a study of academic reform, Hefferlin (1969) has reported:

The most dynamic institutions tend to be those . . . where the junior
faculty appear to have more influence in affecting educational policy
than at other institutions, and where the proportion of tenured faculty is
the lowest [p. 163].

Appointing junior faculty members to major committees, allowing
them to vote, and giving them a reduced teaching load while they are
learning to teach new courses may reduce the exclusive power of an
entrenched oligarchy of elders. They could open the institution to
new ideas and help it retain its vitality.

The task of moving the faculty is, indeed, a crucial factor in innovation—not because the faculty is monolithically opposed to change,
but because there are many sociological barriers to change. Yet
recent experience indicates that faculties can be moved by leaders
who know where their support and opposition rest, and who know
how to use both to develop effective strategies for educational
reform.

Chapter 6

Faculty Cultures and Interdisciplinary Studies

The increase in interdisciplinary study is one important change in American higher education that has particular implications for teaching. New courses and programs of study that focus on social problems, intellectual themes, or human experiences have been introduced at hundreds of schools (Brick & McGrath, 1969; Dressel & DeLisle, 1969). Ethnic studies programs have been instituted in many colleges and universities since the late 1960s (Christensen & Ruyle, 1971). New cluster colleges offer alternative liberal arts curricula that frequently are interdisciplinary (Gaff et al., 1970), and students are increasingly permitted, under independent study or curricula contract arrangements, to construct their own courses or even entire programs from materials and courses not offered by any single department.

The success of these attempts to change undergraduate education rests in large measure upon the willingness and ability of faculty members to move outside their usual intellectual, professional, and social orbits and to work closely with colleagues from other academic disciplines. The analyses presented in this chapter were designed to answer certain questions about the nature and extent of faculty diversity in areas which might affect the success of interdisciplinary courses or programs.

More than a decade ago, C. P. Snow (1959) asserted, on the basis of his own personal experience as both a writer and a scientist, that there were two sharply polarized academic camps—the literary and the scientific. He believed that these two camps were so different that they constituted two separate cultures, with little in common in intellectual, moral and psychological climate. A heuristic use of the concept of academic cultures seems especially appropriate when considering the problems and potentialities of interdisciplinary efforts in colleges and universities. Such a concept implies that there are fundamental differences among professors in various fields, and furthermore that those differences extend beyond subject matter into the realm of values and ideology.

For the purposes of this analysis, all faculty respondents were placed in four cultural groups: humanities, social sciences, natural sciences, and professional-applied fields. These groups constitute and extension of Snow's two cultures to four. The reasons for the extension are both theoretical and pragmatic. Snow himself acknowledged the possibility that social scientists may constitute a third culture; and professional-applied fields represent such a mixed category that it seemed best to deal with them separately. These four faculty groups are examined in terms of educational values, teaching orientation, and life styles in an effort to explore the validity of a separate cultures thesis in understanding how faculty diversity may affect the success of interdisciplinary studies.

EDUCATIONAL VALUES

Educational values were examined by means of further analysis of the data obtained about faculty first and second choices of educational goals for undergraduates. Broad general education was the goal chosen as first or second in importance by 61 percent of the respondents; self-knowledge and personal identity was favored by 44 percent; and knowledge and skills directly applicable to student careers was favored by 31 percent. Other goals received less support.

When faculty responses were sorted according to the four faculty cultures, however, there was little consensus regarding the most important goal of an undergraduate education. While the goal of a broad general education was favored by a majority of faculty members in all cultures, it was most highly favored by social scientists. By comparison, the goal of self-knowledge and personal identity was most highly favored by humanities professors, and the career preparation goal was most highly favored by faculty members in the natural sciences and the professional-applied fields.

To the extent that all of these goals are important for undergraduates, their differential importance to faculty from different dis-

ciplines suggests both potential complementarity and potential conflict in the approach faculty from two or more academic cultures
might take in designing and conducting the same course or curriculum.

Significant cultural variatiaons also appeared in other areas. To determine faculty members' opinions about a number of controversial
incidents that had taken place on college campuses during the time
of our survey, we asked faculty to indicate whether they thought
students and faculty members should be allowed to engage in certain
activities. Table 1 presents their responses by the four hypothesized
cultures. It is interesting that with two exceptions, a majority of the
faculty members in all four categories said that the actions should be
permitted. The two exceptions involved student newspaper articles
on drug use and faculty participation in disruptive activities in the
local community. There was, however, considerable disagreement
among the faculty members in the four categories on most of the
issues. More of the faculty members in the natural sciences and the
professional fields were willing to permit classified military research,
but on all of the other issues faculty members in the social sciences
and the humanities were more permissive. And on the one issue that
poses an almost classic example of academic freedom—the case of
the biology professor speaking out in class in favor of premarital
sex—only about half of the respondents in the natural sciences and
the professional fields indicated their approval.

Another area of inquiry showing variation among the four faculty
cultures is student participation in campus governance. In recent
years there has been considerable pressure to involve students to a
greater extent in the formulation of academic policies, particularly
graduation requirements and curriculum design. In response to a
question on this subject, most respondents were willing to grant
students some voice; only four percent said that students should play
no role in making academic policy decisions. But there were differences between respondents in the four faculty cultures about the
amount of student participation that was desirable. In the social
science and humanities groups, 46 percent would give students
voting rights on committees, whereas in the professional fields only
30 percent would do so, and in the natural sciences only 26 percent
would do so. Thus while a good number of professional and natural
science faculty members would allow student participation in committee discussions, few of them would grant voting privileges.

One possible reason for these differences among faculty cultures
may be that the natural science and professional faculty members

Table 1 Faculty in Favor of Permitting Controversial Activities, by Faculty Cultures, in percentages

Activity	Humanities (N=241)	Social Science (N=172)	Natural Science (N=203)	Professional Fields (N=337)	Total (N=953)
The student government, using student funds, invited a well-known social activist to the campus to speak	94	98	93	85	91
A group of students held an anti-draft protest meeting on campus and subsequently picketed the local Selective Service Board	85	90	74	62	74
An unmarried male and female student couple were found to be sharing the same apartment	72	82	67	55	67
A faculty member conducted classified military research	57	63	70	72	66
A biology teacher spoke out in his class in favor of premarital sexual relations	70	80	54	47	60
A faculty member participated in a nonviolent sit-in demonstration in the administration building	76	72	55	46	60
The student newspaper carried a series of articles on the use of drugs, describing in detail how to use them	54	57	43	36	46
A faculty member organized a Black Power group that engaged in some disruptive activities in the local community	51	68	42	31	45

generally hold the educational goal of acquiring a body of knowledge in high esteem. As a result they may believe, for example, that only a physicist knows what a physics curriculum should include. Educational practices in fields such as business administration and engineering are also determined in large part by standards set and enforced by professional associations; the presence of these external standards may make faculty members feel that student participation in decision making in these fields is neither necessary nor useful.

SUBCULTURES AND TEACHING STYLES

Since major cultural differences in educational values were found, we were interested in seeing whether there were subcultural differences as well. While the questionnaire asked for a good deal of information about faculty teaching orientations, the information focused on here concerns reported classroom teaching practices and attitudes toward students. Responses were analyzed according to sample subcultures. Faculty members in the humanities were subdivided into five groups: English, fine and performing arts, foreign languages, philosophy-religion, and speech-journalism. Those in the social sciences were subdivided into three groups: behavioral science (anthropology, psychology, and sociology), governmental science (economics and political science), and history. Those in the natural sciences were subdivided into three groups: biological science, mathematics, and physical science. And those in the professional and applied fields were subdivided into four groups: business administration, education, engineering, and physical education. That differences in teaching styles exist among these faculty subcultures provides convincing validation of the concept of academic cultures and the pluralistic assumption on which it is based. For example, the first column of Table 2 shows that the most discursive faculty members were found in the philosophy-religion subcultural group, while the least discursive were found in the mathematics and engineering subcultural groups.

It is suggested that these differences may be related to the truth strategies employed by the various fields of study. In a theoretical paper, Thompson, Hawkes, and Avery, (1969) classified fields of study according to the kinds of reasoning they typically employ as "strategies for pursuing and assessing truth." The most highly codified or systematized disciplines (primarily mathematics and the natural sciences) use either scientific or analytic strategies. The less

Table 2 Rank Order of Faculty Subcultural Groups on Selected Variables

Subcultures	Teaching Practices		Attitudes toward Students	
	Discursive	Student-Centered	Skepticism	Permissive-ness
Humanities				
philosophy-religion	1	6	12	3
fine and performing arts	5	2	9	9
foreign languages	6	7	2	5
English	9	8	11	2
speech-journalism	10	14	4	10
Social Sciences				
history	2	10[a]	13	6
governmental science	4	12	8	4
behavioral science	7	4	14	1
Natural Sciences				
biological science	8	3	6	11
physical science	12	9	7	7
mathematics	15	15	10	12
Professional and Applied Fields				
education	3	1	15	8
business administration	11	10[a]	5	14
physical education	13	5	1	15
engineering	14	13	3	13

[a] Both groups received the same score on this variable.

codified fields, generally in the humanities and to a lesser extent in the social sciences, tend to use either direct or inspirational strategies. It would appear from these data that the more codified the knowledge of a field is, the more likely professors are to adopt a tightly focused and structured teaching style; the less codified a field is, the more likely professors are to adopt a wide-ranging discursive teaching style.

Another dimension reflects the extent to which faculty members employ a student-centered teaching approach; that is, do such things as "encourage everyone to get involved in the discussion" and "invite students to help make class plans." As Table 2 indicates, the faculty members in education and the fine and performing arts encourage group participation the most, while those in mathematics encourage it the least.

These differences, again, appear to be related to truth strategies. Professors evidently tend to involve students more in the conduct of courses in those fields that are least codified; in these areas there is more opportunity and perhaps even a definite need for students to codify or structure the knowledge content of the course for themselves. Similarly, professors tend to involve students less in the conduct of courses in more highly codified fields; their classes probably provide less opportunity and less need for students to structure the course content.

An alternative interpretation has been advanced by Holland (1966). In his study of vocational choice, Holland theorized that there are six personality types—realistic, intellectual, social, conventional, enterprising, and artistic—and that people enter fields of study consonant with their personality structures. For instance, individuals with social personalities tend to gravitate toward education and the behavioral sciences; artistic personalities tend to pursue the arts; and realistic personalities are attracted to engineering. Holland's theory may explain why education professors—social personalities—seem to be more student-oriented in their teaching than are professors of engineering, for example.

Whether the primary cause of these differences in teaching style rests with subject matter or with the personalities of faculty, it is interesting to speculate on the implications of such differences for the team approach inherent in interdisciplinary studies. When the subject matter is not codified—as is the case in most new theme or problem-oriented programs—how do faculty from normally highly codified disciplines approach the teaching of it? How do highly discursive and tightly organized faculty work out an experimental course together?

Information about faculty members' attitudes toward students was also obtained and analyzed. The questionnaire contained a series of statements pertaining to several aspects of student life, and respondents were asked to indicate the extent to which they agreed or disagreed with each statement. Five attitudinal dimensions along which faculty members differed were derived from a cluster analysis. The relative positions of the several subdivisional areas on two of these attitudinal scales are included in Table 2.

One dimension describes an attitude toward the academic motivation of students. Sample items from this scale are "students too often want to speculate on important issues before they master the relevant basic facts," "it is generally a better policy to help students acquire a firm foundation in the knowledge of a field before encouraging them to think about the major problems of that field," and "without tests and grades to prod them, most students would learn little." Variations on this dimension are presented in Table 2 under the label "Skepticism." Faculty members in physical education and foreign languages held the most skeptical views; those in education and behavioral sciences held the least skeptical. Since courses in physical education and foreign languages are often required courses and therefore frequently taken by students who have little intrinsic interest in them, it may not be too surprising that instructors in these fields come to adopt skeptical views of students' academic motivation regarding the subject matter and activities offered. These two fields also require the mastery of specific skills, and even when students are motivated, teachers may feel the need for a highly disciplined approach. Whether these same teachers would modify their views if they were teaching very different kinds of courses is, of course, not known.

A second dimension concerns attitudes toward the regulation of the personal behavior of students. This scale is made up of items pertaining to student use of alcohol, school regulations about marijuana, campus dress regulations, curfew rules for women, and premarital cohabitation. Differences between the several subdivisions are shown in the final column of Table 2. Faculty members in the behavioral sciences and English were the most permissive, while professors in physical education and business administration were the least permissive.

LIFE STYLES

One aspect of life style is the kinds of activities a person enjoys. One item in the questionnaire contained a list of several kinds of activities, and faculty members were asked to indicate which were major sources of satisfaction in their lives. As Table 3 shows, the most frequently indicated activity was teaching, with 88 percent making that response. Family relationships was indicated by 79 percent, scholarly pursuits by 62 percent, leisure-time activities by 55 percent, and literature-art-music by 54 percent. Two work-related activities, teaching and research, were more often reported as satisfying than leisure-time activities, responses suggesting that in general these were highly task-oriented people who derive a great deal of intrinsic satisfaction from their work.

Despite this apparent homogeneity, however, the patterning of the

Table 3 Major Sources of Life Satisfaction for Faculty Members, in percentages

Life Satisfaction	Humanities (N = 244)	Social Science (N = 173)	Natural Science (N = 207)	Professional Fields (N = 337)	Total (N = 961)
Teaching	89	88	84	91	88
Family relationships	72	80	77	86	79
Scholarly pursuits (e.g., research, writing)	54	74	72	54	62
Leisure time recreational activities, hobbies, sports	47	50	60	61	55
Literature, art, or music	86	44	49	40	54
Participation as a citizen in affairs in the community	15	23	12	24	19
Participation in activities directed toward national or international betterment	19	24	14	19	19
Religious activities	12	9	13	20	15

major sources of satisfaction revealed differences between the academic divisions. The first three choices of the humanities sample were teaching, literature-art-music, and family; of the natural science and social science sample, they were teaching, family, and scholarly pursuits; and of the professional and applied fields sample, they were teaching, family, and leisure-time activities.

In order to assess a second aspect of life style—political orientation—faculty members were asked to indicate both their party preferences and their positions on a liberal—conservative continuum. Forty-three percent of the sample said they were Democrats; about half that number, 22 percent, said they were Republicans; five percent preferred some other party; and 30 percent considered themselves independents. Democrats were disproportionately drawn from the ranks of the social scientists and were underrepresented among faculty in the professional and applied fields. Conversely, Republicans were most frequently found in the applied areas and were least common in the social sciences.

Thirty-six percent of the social scientists said they were either radical or very liberal, while only 13 percent of the faculty in professional fields chose those designations. On the other hand, 23 percent of the social scientists said they were either moderate or conservative, while 55 percent of those in the professional and applied sample chose those categories. The humanities faculty was similar to those in the social sciences in both party preference and reported liberality, while the natural scientists were similar to those in applied areas.

Spaulding and Turner (1968) found that relationships between discipline and political orientation held up even when they controlled for a number of background factors related to political views, such as parents' political party, and a number of current environmental factors, such as academic rank. They suggested as explanation for these differences that professors in the social science and humanities disciplines, who tend to be Democratic and liberal, are primarily oriented towards social criticism, and that professors in natural science and the professional and applied disciplines, who tend to be Republican and conservative, are largely concerned with the application of knowledge in the business world. They presented evidence that suggested that party preference of the social science and humanities faculty members is affected to some extent by information gained in their academic specialization. Whatever the reasons may be, it seems clear that there is a relationship between academic field and the political orientation of professors.

On another life style dimension—religious orientation—the survey revealed that about half of the college professors generally held a secular viewpoint. Once again, however, differences between academic cultures were found. Nearly half of the social scientists and humanities faculty said they were not affiliated with any church, and about a quarter of each said they were associated with Protestant denominations. The balance were largely Jewish or Catholic. Conversely, almost half of the faculty from the professional fields said they were Protestant, and only about a quarter said they were unaffiliated. The natural scientists fell between these more extreme groups. Similarly, reporting religiosity, 52 percent of the social scientists said they were not religious, compared with 46 percent of those in the natural sciences, 41 percent in the humanities, and 33 percent in applied fields. In general, the ranking of religiosity was similar to that of political liberalism for professors in the four academic divisions.

Thus far it has been shown that there are significant differences among faculty members in different fields of study on such aspects of culture as educational values, teaching orientation, and life style. These differences seem sufficiently great to regard the academic cultures thesis as a useful one for studying faculty. Furthermore, and more importantly, analyses of classroom teaching behaviors and attitudes toward students suggest that there are significant subcultural differences as well. This is not to say that these cultues are discrete; indeed, there are areas of overlap on every item and every scale.

The reasons advanced to account for the existence of faculty cultures fall into two major categories. First is a theory of socialization, which asserts that persons acquire the characteristics of an intellectual culture by being socialized within it. An example would be that social science and humanities professors learn to be people-oriented, critical of the status quo, and tolerant of a wide range of political expression, especially that which attempts to change the status quo, as a part of their undergraduate and graduate education. Second is a theory of attraction, such as that advanced by Holland, which holds that persons with particular patterns of interests and values are attracted to an intellectual culture consonant with their predispositions. This kind of theory holds that persons who are critical, tolerant, and people-oriented are attracted to disciplines in the social sciences and humanities. These alternate explanations for the existence of the cultures have different implications. For example, if one assumes a socialization theory, he might look to future socialization to correct any divisiveness among the disciplines. However, if one holds an attraction theory, faculty cultures would be seen as the result of the differential recruitment of persons with reasonably well-developed, albeit different, personality patterns, leaving little hope that differences among faculty cultures are alterable. Some combination of these two types of theories is probably more accurate than either one alone.

OVERCOMING THE CULTURAL BARRIERS

The conclusion to be drawn from both the present data and earlier research is that current plans for restructuring higher education that rely on interdisciplinary work are not likely to succeed unless educators understand the nature of faculty cultures. Innovators must be attuned to these realities of academic life and set themselves to developing strategies to deal with the several cultures. A few inferences about effective methods for accomplishing this can be drawn from this study.

Recruitment of appropriate teaching faculty—those willing and able to abandon old ways and adopt new ways—poses a serious problem for innovative educational programs. The evidence presented in this paper suggests a major reason: faculty members are ensconced within their respective disciplinary cultures. Heiss (1968) has found that graduate education is quite effective in socializing students into their separate cultures:

> Little in the education of most college and university teachers has prepared them for an interdisciplinary (or a social action) role. Instead, their intense identification with their own discipline renders most scholars uncomfortable and inept outside of its protective confines. If his preoccupation with a special area of interest did not exist before the scholar's formal admission into the academy, everything inside it, from its idioms to its ideologies, constrains him to acquire it [p. 4].

As a result, most interdisciplinary efforts must be staffed by cultural outcasts, faculty who have resisted narrow cultural conditioning or have been exposed to more than one culture. Such persons are not easy to locate, and innovators should probably give a high priority to searching them out.

Interdisciplinary programs typically pass through a period of adjustment. During the early years, members of different cultures express their hopes and expectations only to discover that their general support for interdisciplinary work has masked many fundamental differences. For example, Gamson (1966) has shown that at a small innovative undergraduate college devoted to integrative education, natural scientists and social scientists held conflicting educational views. It is not accidental that meetings of the entire faculty proved to be so stormy that they were abandoned, and business was conducted through divisional meetings. Planners should expect a period of crosscultural exploration complete with misunderstandings before some sort of cultural accommodation can be effected.

Even if the initial period does produce effective working agreements, however, programs may be expected to spawn continuous disagreements around certain key issues, and the alignment of cultures will vary with the issues under consideration. For example, the data suggest that on issues surrounding support and facilities for research and scholarship the social science faculty may align themselves with the natural science faculty, and both may be in opposition to their colleagues in the humanities and applied fields. On issues concerning individual freedom, student-centered policies, and social action, humanities and social science professors may share positions that are opposed to those of their colleagues in the natural sciences and the professional fields. The outcome of such issues may well be determined by the proportion of faculty in each field.

Interdisciplinary efforts are probably more likely to succeed if an attempt is made to merge fields in the humanities and social sciences, than if similar connections are made across the natural sciences, mathematics, and some professional areas such as engineering. This is so for two reasons: more faculty members in the former areas are favorably disposed to interdisciplinary study (a larger percentage thought the proportion of interdisciplinary courses at their schools should be increased, and they reported that in their own teaching they related course content to other fields) and the humanities and social sciences are less codified (their knowledge, methods, and teaching styles are more flexible and can be adapted to new problems and contexts more easily than can the body of knowledge in the more codified areas).

Finally, interdisciplinary centers and educational programs are more likely to succeed if the commonly shared values are kept clearly in mind. While this study has presented evidence that there are average differences between faculty members in different disciplines, these differences are not to be taken as stereotypes of faculty members within the different disciplines. Most faculty members partake from more than one academic culture and few would fit any stereotype exactly.

Furthermore, professors do have common values. Nearly all said they were committed to teaching; the majority felt that scholarly pursuits were a major source of satisfaction in their lives, and most favored a broad general education for their students and valued a climate of freedom for faculty and students alike. While there were differences in the importance that faculty in the four cultures accorded to teaching, research, general education, and freedom, most faculty members generally endorsed such values. It may be that faculty cultures exist primarily because professors choose to realize these values in different ways. Articulation of these common values by leaders of interdisciplinary programs may serve to unite persons from the diverse academic cultures. Knowing that they are working for the same cause may help individuals to rise above their cultural conditioning and live and work productively with their colleagues from other fields.

One might expect that it would be easier to institute interdisciplinary study within each of the cultures than across them. Some institutions have developed subcolleges which, although offering a broad liberal education, emphasize issues that pertain primarily to one culture. For example, Michigan State University has created Justin Morrill College, which has a humanistic emphasis with a major concern for intercultural studies, James Madison College, which emphasizes social science with a focus on policy studies, and Lyman Briggs College, which emphasizes the natural sciences.

There is no guarantee that any of these strategies will work. But it is probable that highly touted interdisciplinary educational programs will fail unless planners understand the pervasiveness of faculty cultures and consciously devise ways to accommodate them to the common goal. A kind of "if you can't fix it, feature it," philosophy may be required. To the extent that innovators do find ways to effect a kind of cultural pluralism—that is, are able to create a climate of respect for alternative habits of mind and style, in which differences are considered complementary rather than in conflict—they may be able to create interdisciplinary programs that are not only successful, but enriched by the very diversity of the faculty cultures.

Chapter 7

Student Voice
and Faculty Response

Perhaps the development in higher education with the most profound long-term implications for the conduct of college and university affairs is the move to redistribute power. Every locus of authority in the operation of colleges and universities has necessarily been involved in this development, seeking to legitimize, expand, or conserve power. The dynamics of the power struggles between governing boards, systemwide coordinating bodies, campus administrations, faculties, students, politicians, and citizen groups have been explored in the recent literature (McConnell, 1971; Metsger, 1970).

One skirmish in this large struggle is the clash between students and faculty. Lunsford and Duster (1971) have argued that students have sought power not simply for its own sake, but to gain more opportunity to change institutional practices and to influence policy on such matters as war, racism, and educational reform. It is obvious, in any event, that students, long excluded from the educational decision-making process, feel that their interests have not been well served. Students have demanded not only less restrictive rules concerning their personal and social lives, but a greater say in the formulation of the rules. They have demanded not only changes in the curriculum, but a stronger voice in planning the changes. They have, in short, claimed the right to equal partnership with other interest groups in determining institutional policies.

It has been said that, with the exception of trustees, the group most resistant to including students in governing bodies is the faculty (Robinson & Schoenfeld, 1970). Our survey attempted to gather some evidence about the attitudes of faculty members toward the inclusion of students in campus governance, and the data has shown that they are generally favorable toward student participation in the formulation of social regulations, but that they are generally reluctant to grant students a similar voice in academic policymaking. The range of individual faculty opinions on both of these issues is wide, however, and the opinions are related to other factors, including educational philosophy, teaching practices, types of contact with students, and general political orientation.

Two-thirds of the respondents were in favor of giving students formal responsibility for formulating social rules and regulations. As Figure 1 shows, 45 percent of them would give students an equal vote on committees, and another 21 percent would give students sole responsibility for their own social regulations. These results possibly reflect the general disinclination of faculty members to be directly involved in matters of dormitory regulation, student discipline, and student government. Since faculty members are primarily responsible

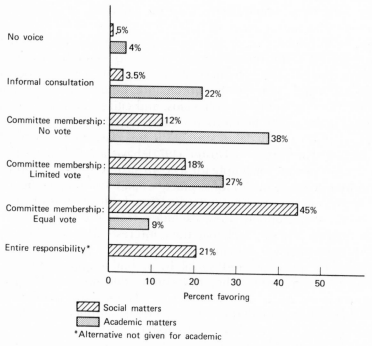

Figure 1. Faculty attitudes about student participation in decisions regarding social and academic policies.

for the intellectual lives of students, they typically hold a laissez-faire attitude toward student activities outside the classroom. In recent years, moreover, professionally trained personnel have assumed many of the duties, formerly performed by faculty members, of supervising and regulating student activities.

Indeed, from the faculty point of view, the concept of *in loco parentis* is a dead issue. The majority of the respondents expressed opposition to dress regulations, curfews in women's dormitories, restrictions on the use of alcohol, and strong college rules against marijuana. And 65 percent reported that they thought a college should not prohibit an unmarried student couple from sharing an apartment.

Faculty response to student participation in setting academic policies is quite another matter. Although only four percent of the faculty members said that students should play no role in formulating such academic policies as graduation requirements, curriculum design, and related issues, Figure 1 makes it clear that most professors are actually reluctant to share their academic power. They are willing to allow informal consultation with students or even allow students to sit as nonvoting members on relevant committees for discussion purposes—60 percent were in agreement—but only 36 percent would accord students a formal role by allowing them to vote on academic policy matters. Moreover, only nine percent would grant students an equal voice with the faculty.

These responses are not surprising. Demands for student participation in academic governance challenge faculty members in their areas of professional competence. Many faculty members feel that in most specialized fields only persons already competent in the areas will know what the curriculum should include. Faculties have fought hard to gain and retain control over these areas; historically, they have stood firm against intrusions from college administrators, boards of trustees, and state governments, and they may be expected to stand firm against encroachment from students.

OPPOSING FACULTY VIEWS

In the present climate of pressure for greater student power in educational decision making, and the likelihood that this pressure will continue, it is important to understand how faculty members react to the possibility of increased student participation in academic policymaking. There are faculty members who support student de-

mands, and there are faculty members who oppose these demands—
what is each group like, and how do they differ from each other?
Perhaps the differences can best be examined by focusing on some of
the characteristics of the two most extreme groups—those 95
professors in the sample who thought that students should be given
an equal vote with the faculty and those 41 professors who believed
that students should have no role at all. Those faculty members
holding more moderate views also appeared to be more moderate in
all of the characteristics considered.

As we might expect on the basis of earlier discussions, the two
extreme groups differ in their beliefs about the nature and goals of
undergraduate education. As Table 1 shows, faculty members who
would share their power with students believe that college should
primarily serve the expressive and self-development needs of
students. When they were asked to indicate the most important goal
of a college education, they most commonly chose the goal of self-
knowledge and personal identity. Very few of them favored such
utilitarian or future-oriented goals as knowledge and skills directly
applicable to student careers or understanding and mastery of some
specialized body of knowledge. Those faculty members who would
give no voice to students, on the other hand, generally chose the
career and specialized knowledge goals instead of the self-knowledge
goal.

The equal-vote group also expressed a more positive view of the
academic motivation of students and their capacity for taking
responsibility for their own actions; 81 percent agreed that class at-

**Table 1   Most Important Goal of Undergraduate Education as Selected by Two
Disparate Faculty Groups, in percentages**

An undergraduate education should help students acquire:	Faculty Groups	
	Equal Vote	No Voice
Knowledge and skills directly applicable to their careers	7	32
An understanding and mastery of some specialized body of knowledge	4	22
Preparation for further formal education	1	7
Self-knowledge and a personal identity	42	7
A broad general education	35	29
Knowledge of and interest in community and world problems	11	3

tendance should be optional, and 73 percent disagreed with a statement that students, without tests and grades to prod them, would learn little. The no-voice group, by contrast, displayed negative attitudes on both counts; only 49 percent agreed to optional class attendance, and only 24 percent disagreed with the statement about tests and grades. On other questions, the equal-voting group took a much more favorable view than the no-voice group toward allowing students the freedom of adults and toward the assumption that students would use this freedom responsibly.

The equal-vote group reported more flexible classroom teaching practices, and they said that they involved their students in their teaching. They were more likely than the no-voice group to endorse the ideas that class assignments should be tailored to the needs of individual students and that students should be encouraged to pursue their own intellectual interests in courses. Far more of them said that they invite students to help make class plans and policy, that they solicit student criticism of their ideas, and that they ask for student evaluation of their courses.

More of the equal-vote group supported academic innovation in their colleges. Most of them thought that emphasis on grades should be decreased and that there should be increases in the proportion of courses directed at contemporary social problems, the proportion of interdisciplinary courses, and the use of independent study. The no-voice group preferred the status quo; their most common response on all these matters was that the situation should remain unchanged.

Considering the differences in these two groups, it is possible to draw this generalization: Faculty members who would share their power with students seem to hold an essentially positive view of students. When these faculty members said that they believe in student academic motivation, value a flexible style of teaching, involve students in their classes, and favor many social freedoms, they seemed to be declaring faith in the ability of students to control and direct their own lives; they were expressing confidence that students can participate constructively in determining the nature of their own education. Faculty members who were most opposed to student participation, on the other hand, tended to believe that external control, motivation, and direction are needed if students are to profit maximally from their education. Each of these opposing views of teaching may be suitable for different kinds of situations, and they may be appropriate for different kinds of students (see Chapter 3).

Political orientation, as well as educational philosophy, is related to faculty attitudes toward student participation. To describe their political position, 78 percent of the equal-vote group indicated liberal, very liberal, or radical (15 percent, in fact, indicated radical). Only 12 percent of the no-voice group chose any of these three terms; 78 percent said that they were either moderate or conservative. From these data, it would appear that faculty members who subscribe to a liberal eduction policy—that is, involving students in academic policymaking—also take a liberal stance in their more general view of society and life.

Additional evidence indicates that the equal-vote group is more politically active. A fair number of them said that the major sources of satisfaction in their lives include participation as citizens in community affairs and in activities directed toward national or international betterment. They appear to share their interest in college politics with students; 76 percent of them said that they had discussed campus issues or problems with at least one student during the previous two weeks, and 21 percent had discussed such matters with five or more students. These responses are significantly greater than for the no-voice group. Collectively, then, the evidence suggests that the minority of faculty members actively committed to co-equal faculty–student determination of academic policies is also concerned with campus reform, which is in keeping with their educational and political philosophies.

Faculty members who favor and who oppose student participation in academic policymaking occupy markedly different statuses in the academy. Those faculty members who are most sympathetic to student demands come largely from the lower ranks, as well as from the less prestigious institutions, and they are more apt to be women. In short, faculty members who hold the least power are the most willing to share that power with students; those faculty members who have acquired the most power are the least willing to share it.

It is noteworthy that the location of faculty who hold extreme views concerning student participation in academic policymaking is similar to the location of faculty who generally favor and generally oppose educational change (see Chapter 5). This suggests that student leaders have been essentially correct in their strategy of demanding partnership in the decision making process itself, rather than settling for specific modifications in rules or procedures. There is little evidence that those faculty who resist student participation in policymaking would accede to student requests for specific educational changes.

To counter any impression that the two groups of faculty members are entirely dissimilar, it should be mentioned that there are many similarities between them. First, the majority of each group thought that effectiveness as a teacher should be very important in decisions pertaining to promotion and salary matters. Second, the faculty members in both groups appear to adhere to what are commonly accepted as responsible teaching practices. Specifically, most of both groups reported that their classroom behavior includes describing objectives at the beginning of class, relating the course work to other fields of study, discussing points of view other than their own, and mentioning reading references for points made. Third, the faculty members in both groups use similar methods in advising students. Nearly all faculty members said that they usually keep office hours, and the majority of them reported that, within the previous two weeks, they had seen students outside of class to discuss academic programs and future careers. None of these comparisons yielded statistically significant differences. In sum, both groups are composed mainly of committed and responsible teachers, even though they differ greatly in their views of the role of students in academic governance.

A LOOK BACK AND A LOOK AHEAD

The issue of student power was brought to the fore during the Berkeley Free Speech Movement in 1964, and the nation's leading universities—Harvard, Columbia, Chicago, Stanford—were rocked by violent student protests, the physical expression of demands for student power. Several reasons have been advanced to explain the unrest in these settings. One theory cites the larger numbers of bright and radical students (Watts & Whittaker, 1966); another argues that student alienation was produced by the large size and multiple missions of such schools (Scott & El-Assal, 1969); and a third theory emphasizes the relevance of protest issues—such as race, war, and academic practices—to centers of academic criticism (Peterson, 1966, 1969).

Through both violent and nonviolent means, students have gained greater voice in many institutions—indeed, many of their gains have come since this survey was conducted. Heyns (1971) concluded that:

... there is no question that student opinion is more systematically collected and heeded than ever before. Areas of final decisionmaking by students may not have enlarged much, but student influence is substantially greater [p. 213].

Blackburn and Lindquist (1970) discovered one major reason for increased student influence. They demonstrated that faculty members vote differently on issues depending on whether students are present or not. The mere presence of students influences faculty members to vote favorably on issues that touch the self-interest of students. This finding suggests that the increase in student membership on policy-making committees, even if the students do not have equal voting privileges (the position supported by the majority of the respondents in this survey) may have increased student influence.

At this time some consequences of student participation are becoming apparent to both its proponents and its opponents. The consequences are now being observed by faculty members, and it appears that the students are neither as good as faculty proponents hoped nor as bad as faculty opponents feared in policymaking roles. Both faculty groups may well see their views at least partially disconfirmed. As faculty members gain more exprience with student participation, their views may be determined less by their educational or political ideologies and more by the actual consequences of student participation in governance on their own campuses.

Yet the dynamic between students and faculty in the continuing struggle for power will doubtless revolve around the two types of faculty members sketched here. If the faculty members favorable to student participation can convince the larger majority of the value of students in committee work, in light of the early experience, the students will probably retain or even expand their power. The faculty members opposed, on the other hand, may try to convince their colleagues that they should take advantage of the decline in student protest to recapture some of the power thay have already lost. Of course, there is also the ever-present possibility that changes in other governing factions might alter this dynamic, either uniting faculty and students around common interests or uniting students with administrators, trustees or legislators in opposition to faculty. The outcome depends a great deal on the role that various segments of the faculty play in coming years.

Chapter 8

Support for Improving Undergraduate Teaching

Teaching and educational change have been the dominant themes of this first study. The results of the study indicate the diversity of faculty attitudes toward teaching and educational change, and the diversity of faculty teaching styles and practices.

While the results of the study relating faculty teaching styles and attitudes to other characteristics are of interest to researchers as they stand, additional steps are necessary to aid educational policymakers and decision makers in their efforts to improve teaching, to encourage innovation and experimentation, and to make effective use of the diversity of faculty talent. To assist educators at the operational level we have made an effort in the individual chapters to translate the research results and point out implications for educational practice.

Before proceeding to the second study we shall briefly summarize some of the major findings and their policy implications. One of the principal findings of this study is that, despite widespread opinion to the contrary, the overwhelming majority of faculty respondents (88 percent) regarded teaching as a major source of satisfaction in their lives. Further, they expressed the feeling that teaching effectiveness is not given the importance that it should be as a criterion of advancement. Although 92 percent indicated that teaching effectiveness should be of high importance in decisions about promotion and salary, only 39 percent believed that it was given that much emphasis in actual practice, and 34 percent believed it was treated as of little or no importance. This wide discrepancy between the desired and the perceived state of affairs suggests the need for a number of institutional and public supports to convince faculty that teaching is indeed regarded as important and that effective performance in this area will be rewarded. A variety of actions have been and are being taken in response to this problem.

Perhaps as a corollary to the importance that faculty believe should be attached to teaching effectiveness, a substantial majority (72 percent) endorsed the idea that their schools should have formal procedures for evaluating teaching effectiveness. Such faculty sentiment has no doubt been a contributory factor in the growing experimentation with procedures for evaluating teaching. Among some of the procedures currently being used are questionnaires, structured interviews, classroom visitations, videotaping and interaction analysis, analysis of curriculum materials and student work, criterion-referenced measures, and pre- and posttest measures of student learning. The most common sources of data on teaching effectiveness include present and former students, colleagues both within and outside the institution, academic administrators, and the instructor himself.

Furthermore, as shown in Chapter 5, there is a considerable reservoir of faculty sentiment favoring innovation and change. Evidence that this sentiment is being translated into action can be found on almost every campus. For example, the Cornell University Center for Improvement of Undergraduate Education recently compiled a directory of more than 3000 innovative projects, classified by discipline and education function. This directory, known as *The Yellow Pages of Undergraduate Innovations,* is available through *Change Magazine.* It includes information about each innovative project and the names and addresses of those responsible for it. Similar lists appear periodically in faculty newsletters issued by teaching and learning centers at a number of colleges and universities.

Since most of these innovations are originated and implemented by individual faculty members in their own courses, their visibility is not high. Indeed, it is not atypical for some of the most successful innovations to be all but totally unknown to the campus community at large. Even those instructors who are engaged in quite similar educational experiments (student contracts, multimedia presentations, auto-tutorial courses, etc.) often do not know about each other's work. This highly individualistic, low-profile approach to educational innovation tends to obscure the amount of innovation occuring on a given campus.

Taken together, the findings of this study indicate that a substantial proportion of faculty favor a more central role for teaching in the reward system, favor formal procedures for evaluating teaching, and favor innovation and change in teaching. This suggests that if under-graduate teaching is to be improved there is a need for administrative and institutional support programs that will assist in translating this sentiment into more widespread practice. In the material that follows we describe a number of examples of such institutional supports for increasing the importance of teaching, and the use of new ways of teaching.

ADMINISTRATIVE SUPPORT

To the extent that administrative policy shapes the priorities and practices of organizations, clear statements at all levels of the organi-zation affirming or reaffirming the importance of teaching may be helpful. Ultimately of course, the effectiveness of such policy sup-ports is determined by the vigor with which they are implemented.

An example of such policy support is found at the University of California in the instructions on appointments and promotions of President Hitch (1969):

> It is the responsibility of the Department Chairman to submit meaningful statements, accompanied by evidence, including evaluations of the candidate solicited from students, concerning the candidate's teaching effectiveness at lower-division, upper-division, and graduate levels of instruction. If such information is not included in the letter of recom-mendation, it is the review committee chairman's responsibility to request it, through the Chancellor.
>
> [The instructions note that] "effective teaching is an essential criterion to appointment or advancement. Under no circumstances will a tenure commitment be made unless there is clear documentation of ability and diligence in the teaching role."

These statements were followed by concurring policy statements by the chancellors of several campuses, academic senate resolutions, and changes in the section of the Faculty Handbook dealing with ap-pointment and promotion. Strict compliance with these policies was delayed until operational procedures for gathering information about teaching effectiveness could be developed and implemented.

Increasingly, however, promotion and tenure committees are requiring greater evidence of teaching effectiveness.

Similar instances of administrative support for giving teaching effectiveness a more central role in the reward system are found in other institutions. For example, in 1970 on the recommendation of the University Senate, the Regents of the University of Minnesota established an Educational Development Program. The university was authorized to devote up to 3 percent of the costs of instruction for this program. The funds are to be used at all levels of the institution for course renewal, innovative teaching, and academic planning.

LEGISLATIVE ACTIONS

Recently a number of state legislatures expressed their concern for the importance of teaching through legislative action. This includes actions such as those of the Michigan and Texas legislatures in prescribing a minimum number of classroom contact hours for university professors (this, of course, does not take into account the importance of out-of-class contact discussed in Chapter 4).

In a more positive vein, the California State Legislature at the urging of the Student Lobby and with the support of Governor Reagan appropriated an additional one million dollars for the University of California 1973–74 budget that was to be used for the improvement of undergraduate instruction. The guidelines for the use of the funds prescribed that at least half the money be used for:

A. *Projects for the evaluation of teaching, and for related programs in which improvement of instruction is sought on the basis of what is learned from the evaluation projects.* It is the intent that if better methods of documenting the quality of teaching are developed, these will be applied in the regular merit and promotion review process, and will thus result in more effective recognition of excellence in teaching.

The remainder was earmarked for:

B. *Summer projects for the improvement of courses, curricula, and instruction, and for the development of new courses.* It is desirable to devote some of the special funding to summer projects of this type because this makes possible planning and revising that could not otherwise be accomplished due to the pressures of the regular academic year. The existence of an incentive to undertake such projects is a visible indication that the activity of planning for better courses and improved teaching is regarded as a worthy alternative to sponsored research during the summer. Awards to faculty participating in summer projects may in no case exceed the equivalent of two months' salary. Students associated in such projects may be paid appropriate stipends.

In selecting summer projects for inclusion in the campus plan, consideration should be given to the magnitude of impact which these project activities will have on students. For example improvement of courses with large enrollments should be given higher priority than improvement of courses with limited clientele.

It is possible that some of the evaluation work in category A may be helpful in identifying prime candidates for projects to be carried out in summer, 1974. Also, some of the summer projects could be the outgrowth of student and faculty consultation during the 1973–74 academic year.

C. *Seminars or other types of special courses for entering undergraduate students.* Here again, the potential magnitude of impact on students should be considered. The goal should be to establish seminars or other special courses which promise to be influential as prototypes for additional courses. Special funding may not be used to hire additional faculty.

These actions of the California Legislature and Regents gave not only policy support for the improvement of teaching, but also operational support by providing funds for specific faculty actions. Similarly, the California State Legislature since 1972 has also provided a fund for innovation and improvement for the California State University and Colleges system.

FACULTY DEVELOPMENT PROGRAMS

Another source of support for increasing the importance of teaching is found in the increasing number of colleges and universities that are instituting so-called faculty development programs. Such programs are designed to raise faculty consciousness about teaching, to extend their knowledge of alternative teaching methods and technologies, and to increase the range and level of their teaching skills. The mechanisms for attempting to bring this about are varied. They include workshops on particular teaching techniques; one-day conferences on topics of general concern, such as examinations and grading; periodic seminar series over a range of teaching-related subjects; and faculty development institutes lasting for several weeks.

The implementation of such programs implies that there is a body of information about teaching and learning that college professors should know about and that the use of such information in their own teaching will increase their effectiveness as teachers.

Many faculty development programs are carried on in conjunction with a teaching and learning center or teaching resources office. Such centers or offices currently exist on at least 75 campuses, including institutions as varied as the University of Michigan, Utah State, and Miami-Dade Community College. Most of the centers were established within the last five years, although the Michigan Center dates back to 1962. While the services offered vary from campus to campus, they typically provide both assistance with traditional teaching activities, such as improving lecture and discussion classes, and assistance in the effective use of some of the more recent teaching technologies such as instructional television, auto-tutorial methods, and simulation games.

In addition to institutional faculty development programs there are a number of cooperative programs between institutions. For example, the Kansas City Regional Council for Higher Education conducts workshops on teaching for faculty in its 18 member institutions, and provides consultants to work with teachers on a continuing basis. The University of Massachusetts at Amherst has developed a teaching clinic program designed for use by several institutions.

THE DISCIPLINARY ASSOCIATIONS

Another line of support for the improvement of teaching is found in the actions of various disciplinary or professional associations. Traditionally such associations engage in activities that will further scholarly knowledge and/or the practice of the profession. In recent years, however, a number of professional associations have established committees or divisions concerned with the teaching of their disciplines. The American Psychological Association has a division on the teaching of psychology and has just instituted a program of teaching awards for college and university faculty in psychology. The American Sociological Association recently established a section on undergraduate education. And at its most recent convention, the American Historical Association gave preliminary approval to the establishment of a third division—to be given equal weight with the divisions on research and professional concerns—whose charge would be "to encourage excellence in the teaching of history in the schools, colleges, and universities." In 1973 the American Geographical Society applied for and received a grant from the National Science Foundation to experiment with training programs for teaching assistants in five universities. In addition, a number of the associations include sessions on teaching as a part of the program of their annual meetings. Such sessions include demonstrations of teaching materials and techniques and symposia or paper sessions focused on particular aspects of teaching a subject. A popular theme for such sessions is often the content and procedures for teaching the introductory course in the discipline.

While most professional associations are relative newcomers to the growing movement to provide support for the improvement of college teaching, a number of disciplines have had for some time a separate association exclusively devoted to promoting excellence in the teaching of that discipline. For example, it is interesting to note that the American Society for Engineering Education has provided a wide range of such support since its inception in 1893. Currently their program includes regional workshops, teaching awards, and publication of the journal, *Engineering Education.* Examples of other professional organizations concerned with college teaching include the National Association of Geology Teachers, the Commission on Undergraduate Education in the Biological Sciences, and the Committee on the Undergraduate Program in Mathematics.

In sum, there are signs of increased support for improving college and university teaching from a number of different sources. State legislatures, administrators, and disciplinary and professional associations give evidence of increased concern not only in their policy statements but in their concrete actions.

In this first study we have examined a variety of faculty characteristics and the ways in which they are related to a number of faculty activities and roles with particular emphasis on their teaching functions. We have examined faculty attitudes toward teaching, the satisfactions they derive from teaching, the relationships they have with students, and their attitudes toward educational change.

In the second study we examine the impacts of different kinds of teachers on different kinds of students using longitudinal data from students as well as data from faculty. These data provide an opportunity to explore further some of the questions examined in the first study, and to examine some of the outcomes of college instruction. We further examine the characteristics of effective teachers and satisfactions they gain from their teaching, replicate and extend the study of out-of-class interaction between faculty and students with data from both sources, and investigate the factors associated with the intellectual development of students, and the academic experiences and changes in students having different patterns of interests.

STUDY II

Faculty Impact
on Students

JERRY G. GAFF
ROBERT C. WILSON

Lynn Wood
Evelyn R. Dienst
James L. Bavry

Chapter 9

A Study of
Educational Outcomes

By what standards may one judge how effective current teaching and learning actually are or how effective they can reasonably be expected to become? Kenneth Eble (1970), Director of the recent Project to Improve College Teaching, has posed the issue in this way:

> During the course of my visits to thirty campuses this past year, I have raised the general question of how good college teaching is and how good it should be with many faculty members and students. To give some definition to these informal inquiries, I have asked, at least half-seriously, how teaching on an individual campus might compare with baseball averages and whether reaching such a level of performance might be a reasonable expectation. Should a college staff maintain a teaching average about as high as a good major league team's won-loss record? Would an individual teacher be a power teacher through the season if he maintained a .300 average in the classroom? Or, calculating the number of outstanding teachers against the total number encountered, would a student feel he was getting fantastic instruction if he broke .400 [p. 2]?

Questions of this sort arise because little is known about the outcomes of college instruction. *Rarely are whole colleges or individual teachers judged on the basis of the contributions they make to the lives of their students.* Rather, colleges are typically evaluated on the basis of the quality of their faculty (e.g., their professional reputation or productivity) and their students (e.g., scholastic aptitude test scores or the proportion of graduates going on to graduate school), which are presumed to be indicative of effective education. Sometimes schools are evaluated by certain attributes of the program, such as the student-faculty ratio or the number of library holdings, which are presumed to facilitate instruction. Similarly, judgments concerning the effectiveness of individual teachers seldom rest on any qualitative changes or quantitative gains shown by their students. More often assessments of teachers' competence are based on their credentials (which is reminiscent of Robert Knapp's comment that a faculty member gets a job by demonstrating that he has been taught rather than by demonstrating that he can teach) or on hearsay evidence from faculty colleagues and students. There is more than a little skepticism that these are sound practices or that they provide the rational basis needed for making decisions concerning educational policies or procedures.

The purpose of this study in general terms is to determine the effects of college teachers on the lives of students by building upon the results of our first survey of faculty members. Since there are many different kinds of teachers, students, and effects, the research question which this study addressed is: What kinds of teachers have what kinds of impacts on what kinds of students in different kinds of educational settings? Different portions of this question will serve as foci of the various chapters that follow. Although answers to the research question will not provide standards of what is possible, they should give a fairly clear view of how good teaching—and learning—actually is, at least in the several schools studied.

Previous studies have found that, in general, faculty are not major sources of influence on the lives of students. Jacob (1957), summarizing the impacts of teachers, cited "evidence that the quality of teaching has relatively little effect upon the value-outcomes of general education . . . so far as the great mass of students is concerned [p. 7]." His added proviso that "*some* teachers do exert a profound influence on *some* students" did little to modify the thrust of his conclusions. Feldman and Newcomb (1969), in their review of the far more extensive body of research literature reported in the next dozen years concerning the impact of college on students, reached a similar conclusion:

> Though faculty members are often individually influential, particularly in respect to career decisions, college faculties do not appear to be responsible for campuswide impact except in settings where the influence of student peers and of faculty complement and reinforce one another [p. 330].

Further, both reviews reach similar conclusions about where teachers do make a difference in the lives of students. Jacob reported that

> Faculty influence appears more pronounced at institutions where associations between faculty and students is normal and frequent, and students find teachers receptive to unhurried and relaxed conversations out of class [p. 8].

And Feldman and Newcomb put it this way:

> The conditions for campuswide impacts appear to have been most frequently provided in small, residential, four-year colleges. These conditions probably include relative homogeneity of both faculty and student body together with opportunity for continuing interaction, not exclusively formal, among students and between students and faculty [p. 331].

The studies in each of these reviews relied very heavily on reports of students to describe the behavior of their teachers, judge the quality of teaching that they received, indicate the relationships they had with teachers, and assess the influence of teachers on their lives. Only a few studies, including the one reported in Study I, have presented evidence obtained from faculty, and virtually none contained evidence drawn from both faculty and students concerning the amount, nature, and outcomes of their relationships.

DESIGN OF THE STUDY

Three distinctive methodological features of this study allow it to go beyond previous research on the outcomes of college education. First, it is interactional; data were obtained from both faculty and students. Not only does the study utilize the self-reports of faculty and students, it also includes data on faculty views of their teaching colleagues and data concerning measured changes in students.

A second feature of the design is that it embraces a long time span. Unlike most prior studies (McKeachie, 1967, 1970) which look for faculty-induced changes in students as the result of a single course, the study reported here employs a time frame which spans the students' entire four years of undergraduate study. Although some may argue that four years is still too short a time to observe the real benefits of a college education, this period is considerably more satisfactory for studying changes than a single academic quarter or semester.

The third characteristic of this design is that it focuses on the kinds of outcomes generally regarded as fruits of a liberal education. Unlike many other studies, such as those summarized by Dubin and Taveggia (1968), where the outcome criteria are scores on final examinations or mastery of course content, we have tried to examine those important, if elusive, outcomes commonly regarded as marks of a broadly educated person.

In an effort to go beyond previous studies of faculty impact on undergraduates, the design of the present study called for obtaining information from both faculty and students, in a diversity of institutions, using a variety of measures of impact. It also called for longitudinal data on students, including some measures of student change.

The study was timed so that, in addition to data from faculty, student data could be used from two longitudinal studies of students being carried on at the Center for Research and Development in Higher Education at the University of California, Berkeley—*The Study of Student Change and Development* under the direction of Paul Heist and *The Study of Differential Education and Student Development* under the direction of Mildred Henry. Eight of the 20 colleges and universities included in those two studies were selected for inclusion in the present study because they encompassed a range of types of faculty, types of students, and institutional settings.

Three coordinated surveys of faculty and students were conducted:

- Faculty members in eight different institutions were surveyed in the spring of 1970 by means of a Faculty Questionnaire.
- Students entering the same institutions were surveyed when they were entering freshmen in the fall of 1966 by the other researchers at the Center in connection with their studies of student development. The freshmen completed two questionnaires, the Omnibus Personality Inventory (OPI) (Heist & Yonge, 1968) and a Freshman Questionnaire.
- In the spring of 1970, when they were graduating seniors students of that initial entering class who remained enrolled in the eight institutions were asked to complete the OPI a second time and to answer a Senior Questionnaire.

The mass of information obtained from these three surveys provides several vantage points from which the impacts of teachers may be observed. Self-reports of students, self-reports of teachers, perceptions of teachers' colleagues, and measured changes in students are all used separately and in combination as evidence concerning the actual effects of teaching and learning.

THE INSTRUMENTS

Four instruments were used to gather data for the study:

- The *Faculty Questionnaire,* a modified version of the instrument used in Study I, was developed for purposes of obtaining a wide variety of information about faculty members' values, attitudes, and activities. As in the first study, the questionnaire contains items for obtaining faculty opinions about appropriate goals for undergraduate education, student participation in policy-making, faculty–student relationships, and a number of controversial campus issues. Additional questions are concerned with faculty members' activities, such as their teaching practices, out-of-class interactions with students, and professional activities. The questionnaire also includes more specific questions about faculty members' self-perceptions of their influence on students in general and their contributions to the development of particular undergraduates.
- The *Omnibus Personality Inventory* (OPI) is a personality measure specifically developed for use with college populations. It contains 390 items that provide measures of 15 different intellectual, social, and emotional dimensions of personality. It has been widely used in studies of students' intellectual and personal growth during the undergraduate years (Chickering, 1969; Heist, 1968; Feldman and Newcomb, 1969). The OPI was administered to students in both their freshman and senior years along with the Freshman Questionnaire and the Senior Questionnaire.
- The *Freshman Questionnaire* contains a large number of items concerning students' family backgrounds, high school experiences, and expectations of college. Additional items concern their educational plans, vocational plans, and attitudes toward a variety of social and political issues.
- The *Senior Questionnaire* contains four types of items. The first type, mainly those items about attitudes and educational and vocational plans, are identical to those on the Freshman Questionnaire. The second type concerns student satisfactions with different aspects of the college experience that paralleled their expectations as freshmen. The third type asks students about many aspects of their college experiences, their peers, their activities, and their relationships with faculty both in general and with individual teachers who had been particularly helpful.

And the fourth type asks students to assess the extent to which they changed in several cognitive and affective ways.

THE MEASURES OF IMPACT

A variety of approaches were used in attempting to measure faculty impact on students. Faculty perceptions of their own impact on students were obtained from a question that asked them to "name one senior to whose educational or personal development you feel you have contributed a great deal." They were also asked to describe a number of aspects of their relationships with that student. Results from this approach are discussed in Chapter 12.

Faculty members' perceptions of their colleagues impact on students were obtained through questions that asked them to name two outstanding teachers and one faculty member "who seems to have *significant impact on the lives of students*." The characteristics, activities, and teaching practices of the nominated faculty are contrasted with those of faculty not nominated in Chapter 10.

Student perceptions of the impact of faculty on them were obtained by asking them to name the teacher of "the most stimulating course" they had taken and by asking them to name "one faculty member who you feel has contributed *most* to your educational and/or personal development." They were also asked to describe a number of aspects of their relationships with that faculty member. The analysis of these student viewpoints is discussed in Chapter 12. In addition, the characteristics, activities, and teaching practices of the faculty members nominated by students are contrasted with those of faculty not nominated by students in Chapter 10. These data were obtained by crossing over to responses to the Faculty Questionnaire.

Our earlier study of faculty as well as much previous research suggested that out-of-class interaction between faculty and students is a crucial aspect of the teaching–learning process. Therefore, faculty were asked to indicate the amount of out-of-class interaction they had with students, and students were asked to report the amount of out-of-class interaction they had with faculty. Chapter 14 discusses the characteristics and activities of both faculty and students that are related to the amount of out-of-class contact they have.

THE MEASURES OF CHANGE

A number of questions in the Senior Questionnaire asked students about how they had changed, both cognitively and affectively during their undergraduate years. In addition, a number of questions in both the Freshman and Senior Questionnaires were the same or parallel in content so that it was possible to determine how their responses had changed over the four years.

These measures of change were related to the previously mentioned measures of impact and are discussed in several chapters. In addition, an analysis was made of the kinds of change which different types of students undergo, and results of this analysis are reported in Chapter 11.

Many people, quite legitimately, raise objections to the kinds of self-reported measures of change just described. They ask: How do you know that the students *really* changed? There is no ultimate answer to this question which would respond to all of the many different things people have in mind when they raise the question. However, as a partial response to the question, we did carry out an analysis that makes use of an independent measure of at least one kind of student change. Chapter 13 reports the results for students who showed a positive change in their Intellectual Disposition as measured by the OPI and the characteristics of the faculty they nominated as having been intellectually influential in their lives. This measure of change is particularly appropriate since it reflects intellectual attitudes and activities that have traditionally been one of the central concerns of undergraduate education.

STATISTICAL TREATMENT OF THE DATA

In the chapters that follow, the differences discussed are all statistically significant at the .05 level of probability, and in most instances at the .01 level. In several of the analyses, the respondents were divided as nearly as possible into thirds on one of the focal measures of impact or change, and the relationships of other variables to these measures were examined with the use of chi-square and Kruskal-Wallis tests. A number of the analyses made use of the correlational approach, since in many instances we were concerned not only with the statistical significance of a relationship but with its relative magnitude as well. For research purposes it is important to determine if a statistically significant relationship exists between variables, but for practical purposes it is also important to know if an educationally significant relationship exists. With large samples, it is possible to find statistically significant relationships that are of little value for suggesting changes in educational practice.

THE INSTITUTIONAL SAMPLE

Three primary criteria were used for selecting the schools: They must encompass a range of types of faculty, types of students, types of social interaction, and types of settings that affect the outcomes of instruction; they must have available longitudinal change data on students; and they must constitute a sufficiently large sample of students and faculty for instances of effective teaching to have occurred, yet be a sufficiently small sample to minimize data management problems. An attempt was not made to obtain a representative national sample of institutions but rather to obtain enough cases of the kinds of effective teaching and learning that we were interested in studying.

Using these criteria, eight schools were selected: two campuses of a major state university, a state college, a subcollege of a state university, two denominational schools, a black college, and a selective independent liberal arts college. Although there is considerable diversity among them, these schools are generally above average in terms of the usual criteria of student abilities and faculty credentials. Following are brief descriptions of the schools as they were at the time of this study:

The University of California at Berkeley. All nine campuses of the University of California were mandated to conduct research, provide graduate and professional education through the doctorate degree, and educate undergraduate students. Undergraduate students were drawn from the most academically talented youth in the state, in most instances those in the top 12.5 percent of their high school classes, and the faculty contained some of the most distinguished scholars in the country. The campus at Berkeley was the oldest, perhaps the most renowned, and one of the largest campuses of the system. It had 28,000 students, 18,000 of whom were undergraduates. About one-tenth of the students lived in university residence halls, and the remainder resided mainly in private homes or co-ops, with some living in fraternities or sororities. The academic senate numbered 1700, and this core faculty was supplemented by many part-time lecturers and teaching assistants. A comprehensive university, Berkeley had over 80 departments and offered a variety of degree programs. The school had a tolerance for social and political criticism and for a diversity of life styles, both of which created a distinctive environment.

The University of California at Santa Cruz. The newest campus of the system, Santa Cruz had adopted several academic innovations. It was organized on the cluster college plan, and at the time of this study had opened six largely residential colleges since 1965. Each student was a member of a college, and each faculty member held an appointment in a college as well as in one of the campuswide boards of study which functioned as academic departments. About 3500 students were enrolled, all but about 250 of them undergraduates, and the school employed 225 faculty. The entire faculty was included in this study, but only students in the second college, Stevenson, were included. This college, which opened in 1966, tended to emphasize study in the social sciences.

Northeastern Illinois State College. A former normal school, Northeastern Illinois State College was transformed into a multipurpose institution in 1967 when it added programs in the liberal arts to existing programs in elementary and secondary education. Located in Chicago, it enrolled 6000 commuting students, about two-thirds of whom were full-time day students and one-third part-time evening students. Its experimental programs involving few and special types of students gave it reason for projecting an experimental image, but most faculty and students worked in quite traditional ways.

Monteith College. Monteith was a small, semiautonomous, degree-granting college within Wayne State University located in Detroit. Since it opened its doors in 1959, it has offered an innovative, integrated, and interdisciplinary approach to general education. It had 35 faculty members, and its 600 students took about half of their work within the college and the rest in other divisions of the university. Although it was a commuting school, its small size, separate physical facilities, and special academic program were designed to create a sense of community similar to that found in residential colleges.

Luther College. A small protestant college situated in Decorah, Iowa, a small midwestern town, Luther College's ties with the church were still quite strong. A recommendation from a student's pastor was required for admission, and courses in religion were required for graduation. Although the bulk of the school's 1000 students were drawn from the region, they were above average in academic ability. The 125 faculty members provided a favorable faculty–student ratio of eight to one.

University of the Pacific. Located in Stockton, California, a city of moderate size, the university had 3000 full-time students and 250 faculty members, and it operated a wide range of liberal arts and professional programs. Its church ties had loosened in recent years, and it had become more experimental. The university was perhaps best known for its pioneering with the cluster college concept; three semiautonomous innovative liberal arts colleges were built during the 1960s. While the entire faculty was included in this study, only students in the original college, College of the Pacific, and in the first cluster college, Raymond College, were included. During the time of this study, College of the Pacific operated a traditional liberal arts program with courses offered in a wide range of departments. Raymond College, which had 200 students and 20 faculty, had an innovative liberal arts program that featured a three-year program, a broad set of prescribed core courses, independent study for all students, and pass–fail grading.

Clark College. A predominantly black college located in Atlanta, Clark was part of a federation of six geographically contiguous predominantly black schools. It was also affiliated with a Protestant church. It served 1000 students, about two-thirds of whom were women, and most of whom were below the national average in academic ability. The program was composed largely of liberal arts programs and teacher education. There were about 100 faculty members.

Shimer College. Shimer was a selective private liberal arts college located in Mt. Carroll, Illinois. It had a faculty of 25, a student body of 400, and a limited but rigorous liberal arts program. The college emphasized group discussion classes, independent study, and comprehensive examinations.

THE FACULTY AND STUDENT SAMPLES

The faculty sample surveyed in all but one of the institutions consisted of all full-time regular faculty members. The exception was the University of California at Berkeley where 12 departments were selected, three from each major area of study—humanities, natural science, social science, and the professional fields. All full-time faculty in these departments were surveyed. The purpose of this approach was to provide a more focused sample than would have been possible with a random sample of faculty across all departments.

A total of 1678 questionnaires were distributed. It was difficult to define precisely who might be a full-time regular faculty member. Responses to the questionnaires, information received from follow-up letters, and subsequent checking with administrative personnel at the institutions, however, uncovered 206 of the sample who were teaching assistants, visiting faculty, administrators, supporting staff, or faculty who were on leave or otherwise not teaching at the time.

These persons were removed from the original group (despite the fact that 76 of them, mostly teaching assistants, had returned at least partially complete questionnaires). Thus, a total of 1472 constituted the final valid sample of faculty. Usable returns were received from 802, or 54 percent, of this group. The range of response rates among the institutions varied from a high of 80 percent at Shimer College to a low of 47 percent at Berkeley. (The number of questionnaires distributed and returned and the rate of return for each institution are given in Appendix II.)

Special mention must be made of the spirit of the times when these data were being gathered. The time was spring 1970; the nation had experienced yet another year of widespread campus disturbance, and many academics felt that there was increasing repression by civil authorities. The existence of undercover agents on campuses became common knowledge; several public and private organizations had collected vast amounts of information on large numbers of people; and these data banks were exposed as having been used against certain individuals. The culmination of the unsettling year occurred in May when the United States invaded Cambodia; campuses all across the nation erupted, and students at Kent State and Jackson State Universities were killed, as civil authorities attempted to put down the protests. It was hardly an optimal time to field a questionnaire to faculty members.

The effects of these events can be observed in the discrepancy between the 54 percent response rate obtained here and the 70 percent obtained in the 1968 survey reported in the first study. The questionnaires were comparable in appearance, length, and content. Furthermore, exactly the same procedures were used in each study. An introductory letter, along with a copy of the Research Reporter (a publication of the Center for Research and Development in Higher Education at the University of California, Berkeley, containing brief reports of research findings), was sent to each person in the faculty sample to introduce the Center and describe this project to him. Shortly thereafter, a questionnaire with a covering letter was sent. About a month later, a short follow-up letter with an enclosed stamped postcard, on which the faculty member was asked to indicate whether he intended to complete the instrument, was sent to all nonrespondents.

The questionnaires were mailed during February and March 1970 so that they would arrive about one month after the start of each school's spring term; follow-up letters were mailed during March and April. Early in May it became apparent that additional steps would have to be taken to obtain an acceptable response rate. A telephone follow-up was begun, and most of the nonrespondents at two schools had been contacted when the post-Cambodia protests broke out. That situation effectively aborted the telephone follow-up, as the request to complete a questionnaire was too trivial a matter to discuss when respondents were concerned with an international war, domestic instability, and in some cases the physical safety of their students and themselves.

Because the protests were an important phenomenon in their own right, and because they affected faculty–student relationships, a special one-page questionnaire designed to elicit faculty views of the protests was prepared and distributed to everyone in the sample in mid-May. A duplicate copy of the original faculty questionnaire was included in the envelopes sent to all the faculty members who had not yet returned the questionnaire. Given the spirit of the times and the variety of standard and makeshift follow-up procedures, the response rate, though low, seemed quite an achievement.

The two student samples presented contrasting difficulties to the researchers who collected that data. All freshmen entering seven of the schools in the fall of 1966 and a random sample of two-thirds from Berkeley were selected for study, and 4815—virtually all of them—completed the questionnaires.

The senior sample proved more difficult to obtain for a variety of reasons. Omitting from calculations one school that lacked complete records on its students, only 53 percent of the initial student sample were still enrolled at the same schools four years later. This large dropout rate is fairly standard for most colleges and universities (Summerskill, 1962). But discovering where the remaining students were living presented another problem; and gaining their cooperation to complete a lengthy questionnaire and personality inventory, especially at that turbulent time, was not an easy task. In all, 1475—or 61 percent of those remaining in school—returned usable questionnaires. This group, the 1475 students for whom a complete set of freshmen and senior data were available, constituted the student sample for this study. The institutional response rate among seniors ranged from a high of 75 percent at Stevenson College at Santa Cruz to a low of 35 percent at Clark College. (Information about the freshmen and senior samples, including rates of response for each institution, is given in Appendix II.)

This particular sample of students possesses certain advantages for studying the outcomes of teaching and learning. They constitute a large number of persons for whom both freshman and senior data are available, and as seniors they have an excellent vantage point from which to assess aspects of their college experience. On the other hand, this sample fails to include not only the nonrespondents but also the relatively large number of students who dropped out of school or those who transferred to other institutions. For these reasons, the sample is not likely to shed much light on the "failures" of education, but it should reveal differential positive effects of teaching among students who remain enrolled for four years in the same college.

Chapter 10

The Characteristics of Effective College Teachers

Throughout history many quite disparate images of especially effective or impactful teachers have emerged. While they are best known by their real or fictional stereotypes, most of the types are to some degree represented among the faculties of American institutions of higher education today. Consider, for example, Aristotle or the Hindu guru with their bands of devoted students. While the guru is rare in modern-day education, he does appear intermittently on the faculties of American colleges and universities, where his often unorthodox methods and relationships with students, as well as the content of that which he professes, attract bitter controversy. Or consider another type, the brilliant lecturer, the eminent university professor known universally for his contributions to a discipline. His teaching style—at least among undergraduates—is largely limited to the formal presentation of course materials, often from a lectern, to a vast auditorium of students, and he is rarely engaged in any personal, or even intellectual, exchange with them. Another type is represented by the famous Mr. Chips, living examples of whom are most typically found in small liberal arts colleges, which in many ways are natural extensions of the prep school setting. There is a widespread nostalgic support for the low-keyed, no-nonsense approach to education taken by this type of influential teacher as well as for the personal, holistic, and continuous relationships that he has with generations of college students. And, of course, there are the subject-matter and the student-centered teachers portrayed in Chapter 3.

Given these disparate styles, which have been thought at one time or another to exemplify the outstanding teacher, it would be unreasonable to expect faculty to unanimously agree on a single type as the only especially effective or impactful teacher. Given, too, the diversity of learning styles and needs of students, it would be equally unreasonable to assume that only one kind of teacher would be perceived by all students to be especially effective.

Yet, despite the diversity of potentially effective teaching styles that might be found to characterize faculty, it is to be expected that faculty who stand out in the minds of their students and their colleagues will have much in common. Indeed, a substantial research literature has accumulated since as far back as 1929 (Remmers), and it has grown remarkably in recent years as a result of intensified interest in defining the characteristics of effective teachers (McKeachie, 1969; Thielens, 1971; Hildebrand, Wilson, & Dienst, 1971).

Although most studies of effective teaching have reached rather similar conclusions about the defining characteristics of outstanding college teachers as described by students (they often include thorough knowledge of subject matter, skill in presentation, friendly relationships with students, and enthusiasm), faculty critics suggest that this method of using student ratings yields a measure of popularity rather than of effectiveness. With this criticism of past research in mind, it is relevant to ask: How do those faculty who are nominated by college seniors as their most effective teachers describe themselves? How do they differ from their colleagues? To what extent are the characteristics of student-nominated faculty the same as or different from faculty who are nominated by their colleagues?

IDENTIFYING EFFECTIVE TEACHERS

Faculty members in this study were asked to name two colleagues at their institutions whom they regarded to be outstanding teachers as well as one teacher whom they regarded as having significant impact on the lives of students.

An effective teacher, as seen by his colleagues, is defined here as a teacher who received nominations as either outstanding or impactful from two or more of his colleagues. The criterion of two or more nominations was employed in order to increase the reliability of the measure by eliminating those teachers who received a nomination from only one other teacher; the likelihood of educationally irrelevant criteria (such as friendship, kinship, or research partnership) being applied would seem to be greatest in such instances. The questionnaire responses of the 137 faculty who received nominations from two or more colleagues were contrasted with those of the 525 faculty who received no nominations from any colleague. The 140 faculty who received nominations from only one colleague were not included in this analysis.

College seniors in this study were asked to name the teacher who had taught the most stimulating course they had taken during their college careers as well as the one teacher who had contributed most to their educational and/or personal development.

An effective teacher, as seen by his students, is defined here as a teacher who received nominations as either most stimulating or contributive by two or more of his students. Again, the criterion of two or more nominations was employed in order to increase the reliability of the measure by eliminating those teachers who—however much impact they might have had on a single student—might have been nominated for idiosyncratic reasons. The questionnaire responses of the 97 faculty who received nominations from two or more students were contrasted with those of the 609 faculty who received none. The 96 faculty who received nominations from only one student were excluded from this analysis.

The two nomination groups—the colleague-nominated and the student-nominated—are by no means mutually exclusive. Indeed, there is considerable overlap between the two. Of the faculty receiving two or more nominations by colleagues, 51 percent received nominations by students as the teachers of the most stimulating classes they took during their college careers, and 48 percent received nominations by students as the teachers who had contributed most to their educational or personal development. On the other side, of those faculty receiving nominations by two or more students, 57 percent received nominations by colleagues as outstanding teachers, and 37 percent received nominations by colleagues as teachers who had significant impact on the lives of students. As these figures indicate, there is substantial agreement between students and faculty as to who are the especially effective teachers on these eight campuses. And these findings are in agreement with the findings of an earlier study of best and worst teachers on the campus of a major state university (Hildebrand, Wilson, & Dienst, 1971), where considerable consensus among students and faculty nominators also was found.

FACULTY SEEN AS EFFECTIVE

The two groups specifically under consideration here are those nominated by colleagues and those nominated by students. When the distinctive characteristics of the colleague-nominated group were compared with the distinctive characteristics of the student-nominated group, a number of similarities were found. These similarities constitute characteristics that are assumed for the purposes of this study to represent the general characteristics of effective faculty. Characteristics that apply only to the colleague-nominated group and only to the student-nominated group will be treated separately.

Two analyses were made. The first analysis compared faculty nominated by two or more colleagues ($N = 137$) with faculty not nominated by any colleagues ($N = 525$). The second analysis compared faculty nominated by two or more students ($N = 97$) with faculty not nominated by any students ($N = 609$). Variables that were significant in both analyses or that were not significant in both analyses have provided the basis for a discussion of the general characteristics of effective faculty.

Differences That Do Not Make a Difference One of the most surprising findings of both analyses is how little those faculty nominated by students and colleagues as effective differ from their fellow teachers on a number of attitudes, values, attributes, and behaviors that were expected to be related to effectiveness. As a group, effective faculty express a wide diversity of opinion on such questions as the amount of personal freedom that should be accorded students in matters of dress and demeanor, the extent to which students should participate in academic decision making, and the extent to which colleges should tolerate various forms of political activity and protest by faculty and students. Common to all these questions is a radical to conservative sociopolitical dimension that was found to be related to a number of attitudes toward teaching and educational change in the first study. This dimension was expected to be associated with perceptions of faculty as impactful, especially by students.

We anticipated, for example, that students would tend to identify most strongly with those faculty who were closest to themselves in chronological age and most liberal in sociopolitical ideology. In spite of the troubled times during which this study was conducted, however, this was not found to be the case: Faculty nominated by students came from among the oldest as well as the youngest of faculty and from among the conservative as well as the radical. While some diversity of sociopolitical attitudes and activities were expected to characterize both students and faculty, it is now evident that a much too homogeneous and radical picture of students in 1970 was held by the research staff. In fact, the data show that our sample of students on eight diverse campuses was divided almost equally between radicals and liberals, on the one hand, and moderates and conservatives, on the other. This reflects in part the diversity of institutions included in the study, of course. It also suggests, however, that despite the radicalized image of American college students that had become crystallized in the mass media, there was still considerable political diversity—and substantial numbers of conservatives—among American college students generally. By way of contrast, faculty at these same eight institutions tended to characterize themselves as much more homogeneously liberal than did students, although they showed considerable variability in their actual support for specific issues or activities that are politically relevant. This would suggest, too, that the meaning of such political labels varies both over time and among different social groups.

Differences That Do Make a Difference   While the differences that do not seem to make a difference are surprising, they are also in many respects encouraging. Individual characteristics, such as age, political designations and affiliations, and sociopolitical attitudes and ideologies, are relatively difficult to change. They are also in large part educationally irrelevant. Since the major purpose of this study has been to discover how teachers who are perceived to make a difference seem to go about making that difference, it is both instructive and gratifying that the factors that distinguish impactful faculty from their fellow teachers appear to be grounded as much in what they *do* as in what they *think*—in how they *act*, especially vis-à-vis students, rather than what they *believe*. It seems likely, therefore, that an analysis of characteristics that do make a difference might suggest a model of effective teaching, aspects of which could be adopted by individual teachers or by an entire college faculty in an effort to improve college teaching.

Faculty reported by both students and colleagues to be especially effective do, for example, evidence a greater commitment to undergraduate teaching. In significantly greater numbers they registered preferences for teaching to engaging in research and for the teaching of undergraduates to the teaching of graduate students (see Table 1).

They also significantly more often named two seniors whom they had found especially enjoyable to teach, suggesting that they more often found teaching enjoyable generally, since there is little reason to believe that nominated teachers should be less reluctant to name students than their colleagues who were not nominated. Effective teachers also scored significantly lower on an attitudinal scale measuring a positive orientation toward research (the scale contains items largely justifying research as contributing to the improvement of teaching). This further suggests that the primary commitment of especially effective teachers is to the teaching rather than to the research aspect of the academic role. (Technical information about faculty scales can be found in Appendix II.)

By their own report, effective faculty also behave quite differently vis-à-vis their students, both within and especially beyond the classroom. Within their classrooms, impactful teachers are more likely to strive to make their course presentations interesting than are their colleagues (see Table 2). Specifically, they more often reported using stories and analogies to make a point and sharing examples from their own experiences or research. On the other hand, effective teachers have not been found to be any more or less likely than their colleagues to be either highly organized or highly discursive in their presentation of course materials. It seems to matter very little whether an instructor prepares and distributes course outlines, describes objectives, or uses detailed notes in class, for example. Nor does it seem to matter whether he discusses a wide variety of points

Table 1   Faculty Commitment to Teaching by the Number of Nominations Received from Students and Colleagues as Effective Teachers, in percentages

	Nominations by Colleagues		Nominations by Students	
	Two or More	None	Two or More	None
Prefer teaching to research	83	67	80	67
Named two seniors as having been especially enjoyable to teach	73	48	81	49
Research orientation:				
Low scores	40	27	39	27

Table 2   In-Class and Out-of-Class Behaviors of Faculty by the Number of Nominations Received from Students and Colleagues as Effective Teachers, in percentages

	Nominations by Colleagues		Nominations by Students	
	Two or More	None	Two or More	None
Interesting presentation scale:				
High scores	41	24	32	26
Contemporary issues scale:				
High scores	51	29	52	32
Out-of-class interaction scale:				
High scores	55	26	54	30

of view, relates the course work to other fields of study, or discusses the origin of ideas introduced in his classes.

In keeping with their attempts to be interesting, impactful teachers are also significantly more likely to talk with students about a variety of contemporary issues of importance, and even urgency, to young adults. In both the colleague- and student-nomination analyses, more than 50 percent of the faculty nominated as most effective scored high on a scale concerning the frequency with which they discuss with students such topics as sex and morality, the use of drugs, student activism or protest, the draft, and emerging life styles. Fewer than one-third of the faculty not nominated reported such frequent discussions of this type with students. "Rap sessions"—whether they occurred inside or outside the classroom—are evidence of the impactful faculty's greater involvement with students and their greater concern for issues of paramount importance to students. Here it should be recalled that effective faculty do not, however, differ appreciably from their colleagues in their attitudes toward such contemporary issues. Thus, in talking about such issues as drugs and protests, it may well be that to some extent the medium is the message; that is, the key to having an impact on students may well be a teacher's willingness to openly discuss such issues, rather than the extent to which he agrees with students concerning the subjects discussed.

There is an exception to this general finding, however. Apparently, in times of immediate and visible political crises, the political attitudes and actions of faculty do become important. On those campuses where faculty indicated there had been a student protest, effective faculty not only more often discussed the protest issues with students informally, but they also more often took actions in support of the student protests than did faculty not nominated by students or colleagues. Interestingly, though, those faculty who were not nominated by either students or colleagues did not more often take actions in opposition to the protest—they simply took less action of any kind.

But the single biggest difference between effective faculty and their colleagues was the extent to which they interacted with students outside the classroom. As in the first study, faculty respondents were asked to indicate how many times they had out-of-class discussions with students in several areas ranging from course work to personal problems (see Chapter 14). The close relationship between having an impact on students and interacting frequently with them outside the classroom can be seen in Table 2. It seems clear that a college teacher's chance of being regarded as especially effective is immeasurably increased by the extent to which he interacts with students beyond the classroom. Given the importance of such contact to perceptions of effectiveness, the data would seem to indicate that much effective teaching—impact—may take place outside the classroom.

Making a Difference, Self-Perceived   If making a difference can be thought of in some sense as its own reward, then effective teachers would appear to reap a greater sense of accomplishment from their teaching efforts. Effective teachers seem to feel a sense of educational potency; for example, they seem to be aware of the impact they have on students in general, and they are more likely to name a college senior to whose educational or personal development they feel they have contributed a great deal. Forty-four percent of the student-nominated faculty scored high on a scale of *Self-Perceived Influence,* which measures the extent to which faculty think they have an impact on students' personal philosophies, decisions about careers or majors, and appreciation of the values and methods of scholarly inquiry; only 27 percent of the faculty not nominated felt that they had as much influence on students generally. Comparable differences have been found between the faculty receiving two or more nominations by colleagues and those receiving none. Similarly, 78 percent of the student-nominated and 68 percent of the colleague-nominated faculty named college seniors to whose development they had contributed a great deal, whereas only 48 and 49 percent of the faculty not nominated by either felt that there were such students or were willing to name them. Because the faculty not nominated have significantly less out-of-class contact with students, it may be that they often do not know their students well enough to be able to assess their own impact on them.

These major characteristics represent ways in which teachers make an impact on students and in which effective teachers become visible to their colleagues. Moreover, it should be pointed out that they are for the most part descriptive of what an impactful teacher does or says he does—not what he thinks. The observation is encouraging: It is much easier for a teacher to change what he does than to change what he is. This finding suggests that college teaching can, in fact, be improved—improved in ways that impress one's students and colleagues, at least—by upgrading certain key teaching practices.

It is also important to note that, for the most part, the characteristics that have emerged are educational characteristics. Surely a teacher is more likely to get his point across if he is interesting in his presentation of it than if he is matter-of-fact or just plain dull. While showmanship can undoubtedly be carried too far, it seems unlikely that any reasonable educational critic would feel that to strive to be interesting is pedagogically irrelevant or unsound. A major part of teaching and learning may involve successful modeling or identification; likeable, interesting, and available teachers are undoubtedly more powerful and acceptable models. Certainly, too, a teacher can expect to have greater impact on his students if he has more contact with them than if he has less. Again, while it is no doubt possible to carry chumminess too far, it seems difficult to believe that anyone would judge that interacting with students outside the classroom is a poor educational strategy.

No doubt, too, a teacher's effectiveness can be enhanced by his having good rapport with his students, by being able to discuss issues most germane to their own immediate lives. While it may not be possible to reduce all education to the level of rapping, there is no reason to suppose that there is a negative relationship between a teacher's willingness to talk with students and his ability to communicate the intricacies of quantum mechanics or Dante's *Divine Comedy,* and it makes sense that there would be a positive connection between them.

ADDITIONAL CHARACTERISTICS OF COLLEAGUE-NOMINATED FACULTY

There are a few characteristics of teachers who are nominated by their colleagues as outstanding or impactful that are not characteristic of faculty nominated by students. The most interesting thing about these characteristics as a whole is that they appear to be less directly relevant as indices of effective or impactful teaching performance.

Faculty members who are perceived by their colleagues to be outstanding or impactful tend to be older, to occupy the highest academic ranks, and to have had more teaching experience both within their present institutions and throughout their careers. It appears that faculty nominees were named, at least in part, because they are more visible to their colleagues, whether for their teaching excellence or for some other reason. Another characteristic that appears to weigh heavily in colleague judgments is a teacher's research or scholarly activities. Although faculty nominated by both students and colleagues tended to score low on an attitude scale measuring their orientation toward research, colleague-nominated teachers tended to be more active in their scholarly professions, more often having delivered papers at professional meetings than those faculty not nominated by their colleagues. In contrast, faculty nominated by students were less actively involved in research and professional activity by this same measure than were those not nominated by students. This suggests that to some degree colleagues take scholarly activity into account in the nomination of impactful faculty, perhaps using as one criterion of an outstanding teacher that he remain active in his field. Hayes (1971) found, in fact, that department heads' judgments of teaching quality tend to be associated with their judgments of research ability. Students, on the other hand, do not use this as a positive criterion of good teaching; indeed, they may not even be aware of their teachers' scholarly or professional activities.

Not all the characteristics that differentiate colleague-nominated faculty from those nominated by students are irrelevant to effective teaching, however. Faculty nominated by their colleagues also differed in some of their attitudes regarding a teacher's personal responsibility for students. For example, 60 percent of the faculty nominated as outstanding or impactful by colleagues agreed that "if a student fails a course, it is at least partly the fault of the teacher," whereas only 46 percent of the faculty not nominated shared that position. Perhaps more important, it seems likely that impactful faculty more often communicate such ideas to their colleagues. Fifty-nine percent of the colleague-nominated faculty and only 48 percent of the faculty not nominated said that it was quite descriptive or very descriptive of their departments that "faculty exchange ideas regarding their teaching." This latter finding suggests, too, that the departmental as well as the institutional climate may be an important factor in the promotion of effective teaching. Where concern for and discussion of teaching is the norm, the chances that individual teachers will practice effective teaching, or at least will make efforts in that direction, may be substantially increased.

ADDITIONAL CHARACTERISTICS OF STUDENT-NOMINATED FACULTY

Student-nominated faculty differ in only one characteristic from teachers also nominated by their colleagues. Teachers nominated by students tend to devote class periods to discussing protests that have taken place on their campuses. Seventy-two percent of the student-nominated faculty responded to this issue in this way, whereas only 50 percent of the faculty not nominated by students did so. This may suggest to the skeptic that students perceive as outstanding teachers those who are easily persuaded to turn over their classes to politics or current events. Recalling the politically troubled spring of 1970, however, it may also be said that impactful faculty—who have been shown to more often discuss such issues generally with students—regarded the crisis as sufficiently important to preempt scheduled discussions of regular course materials. While faculty nominated by colleagues did not more often turn over class periods to such discussions than those not nominated, they did report that they more often discussed protests with their colleagues informally and more often served on faculty or administrative committees that dealt with protests. It should be recalled that they also, along with the student-nominated faculty, more often took actions in support of protests. Student-nominated faculty tended to interact with students in a political crisis whereas colleague-nominated faculty interacted with one another. Hence, through careful analysis of a single crisis situation one is able to gain clues as to a major cause of a teacher's receiving nominations from either of the two groups: frequent and close association, communication, and interaction between the nominating group and the nominee.

CONSENSUS AND DISSENSUS

Despite wide variations in personal characteristics and teaching styles, faculty who are perceived by their students and their colleagues to be especially effective or impactful share a number of characteristics: They share a greater commitment to teaching generally; they strive to make their courses interesting; and they interact more with students and have greater rapport with them. It is also apparent that some— but certainly not all—of the criteria employed by colleagues in making such nominations are not directly relevant to effective teaching. That a student-nominated teacher interacts more with students than does a teacher not nominated is understandable. His interaction could be expected to act both as a cause of his receiving nominations (he is better known to his students) and as a criterion by which he is judged to be effective or impactful. That a colleague-nominated teacher interacts more with his fellow teachers, however, would seem to explain only *how* he comes to be nominated (he is better known to his colleagues), but not *why* he is seen to be outstanding or as having significant impact on the lives of students.

Of the two types of nominations, those made by students seem to be somewhat more squarely based on educational criteria. While faculty utilize the same educational criteria as do students in making their nominations, they also seem to take into account some criteria—such as age and rank, research productivity, and the like—that appear to have little educational relevance. They also take into account factors that make a teacher's concern for students and for the education process *visible* to them, through participation in faculty committees, informally discussing issues relating to teaching with colleagues, and just generally making themselves better known to their colleagues than do the faculty not nominated. This would suggest that the use of only colleague nominations or ratings as the bases of teaching evaluations might be more suspect as popularity contests than those derived from students alone.

Overall, it is important to note the basic consensus between students and faculty as to what some of the characteristics of effective teachers are. This finding suggests the desirability of utilizing both colleagues and students in identifying effective teachers and in assessing teaching effectiveness more generally. By using the judgments of both groups, it may be possible to overcome some of the faculty resistance to teacher evaluation, and we may better understand which faculty meet the criteria of effectiveness for both their colleagues and the students they teach.

Chapter 11

Behind the Faces in the Classroom

Teachers—even outstanding teachers—face the constant challenge of providing instruction that meets the needs of a wide range of students. Prerequisites to their meeting that challenge are awareness of who their students are and knowledge of the different kinds of students present in their school and classrooms.

Information about students currently available to professors is limited. Perhaps the most common sources are comments of students in class and discussions with students outside of class, but as will be shown, only certain kinds of students make their concerns known to teachers in these ways. The impression has been given, especially by the mass media, that there was one typical kind of student during the late 1960s, a radical protester. Earlier student stereotypes were the older, serious-minded ex-GI of the late 1940s and the early 1950s and the raccoon-coated, charleston-dancing sport of the 1920s. Academic folklore concerning the desirability of bright, highly motivated students also provides little insight into the range of student motivations.

A good deal of research has attempted to specify the diversity and distribution of student interests, and several schemes for categorizing students—some theoretical and others empirical—have been developed. Clark and Trow (1960), for example, have discussed four types of student subcultures: the academic, the nonconformist, the collegiate, and the vocational. Holland (1966) has described six personality types: realistic, intellectual, social, conventional, enterprising, and artistic.

This chapter attempts to go beyond previous research and show the ways different kinds of students have benefited from various aspects of the academic program and how a wide range of students relate to faculty members. Several orientations of college students to school will be described and related to the academic experiences and educational outcomes of students. It is hoped that these data will reveal what is behind the faces in the classroom, and that they can suggest ways in which both whole colleges and individual teachers may better meet the needs of a diversity of students.

Nine scales, each reflecting a separate dimension of student life, were derived from a factor analysis of items on the senior questionnaire. Each dimension combines responses to such items as students' interests while in college, the interests of their closest friends, their activities in college, and their expected interests after graduating. These categories are not regarded as mutually exclusive, and each senior is scored on each dimension, a procedure that reflects the fact that each person has multiple interests and engages in several kinds of activities. While technically students' scores on these dimensions run from high to low, the names of the dimensions are attached to the high ends of the scales. The nine scales are:

Intellectual. Students who score high on this dimension have pursued intellectual interests independently during their college days; they expect intellectual interests to be an important part of their lives after college; and they have read large numbers of books for their own pleasure, apart from assigned reading. Although they expect to obtain advanced degrees, they have spent no more than average amounts of time studying for courses. They enjoy pursuing ideas, but mainly only those ideas in which they are personally interested.

Academic. Students scoring high on this dimension are academically oriented, but they seem to be motivated more by external factors, especially grades, than by the sheer joy of learning. They report that they have been heavily involved in intensive scholarship in their academic specialties, that they have been committed to achieving good grades, that they have studied many hours each week and have tried not to waste time, and that their closest friends are also interested in academic course work. They seek advanced degrees, but their academic interests seem to be motivated largely by extrinsic factors; they have read fewer books outside of class than have the students high on the *intellectual* dimension.

Activist. This dimension, unlike all of the other dimensions, is defined solely in terms of behavior. Students who score high on this scale have engaged, to a greater extent than their peers, in nonviolent student-protest activity. Specifically, they have participated in rallies to protest public policy; they have donated money, picketed, marched, canvassed, or petitioned for a cause; or they have worked more actively for a social cause. These students are also intellectually oriented, as evidenced by the fact that they expect to earn higher degrees, and they have read large numbers of books outside of class. Their major concerns, however, seem to be focused on off-campus social and political events, as they have spent only average amounts of time studying for courses.

Vocational. Students scoring high on this dimension, like the students high on the *activist* dimension, have set their sights off campus, but for a different reason: They are preparing for their postcollege careers. They have been concerned with acquiring knowledge and skills with which to make a living; they have been enhancing their upward mobility via college; they are more definite in choice of occupation; and they expect vocational pursuits to be important after their schooling. Students scoring high on this dimension are neither more nor less likely than their fellow students to seek advanced degrees. They have read fewer books than students scoring low on this scale, but they have dutifully spent more than average amounts of time studying. They appear to be working primarily to acquire the skills and the degrees that will certify them for good jobs after they have left college.

Artistic. Students who score high on this dimension say that esthetic interests and cultural pursuits have made major claims on their time. Their friends are involved in artistic endeavors; individual artistic or literary work has been an important source of satisfaction during school; and artistic interests are expected to be important in their future lives. These students, like students high on the *intellectual* and the *activist* dimensions, have read more books, but they have more modest aspirations toward advanced degrees.

Hip Nonconformist. Students who score high on this scale say that they, as well as their friends, read underground magazines and are interested in drugs. They have read more than an average number of books for their own pleasure. These students, contrary to the beliefs of some critics, appear to be not so much anti-intellectual as anti-academic; in this respect their attitudes are similar to those of students high on the *intellectual* and *activist* dimensions and indeed to some extent are represented among them.

Athletic. Participation in sports or athletics has been a major interest of students scoring high on this dimension. They have read many hobby or sports magazines; they expect athletics to be of major interest to them after graduation; and their friends are also involved in athletics. As the stereotype of campus athletes suggests, these students have read fewer books than average for their own pleasure; they have spent somewhat less time than average studying; and they have only average expectations about obtaining higher degrees.

Social. High-scoring students on the social dimension indicate that being socially active has been a major interest during college. Parties and social life have been important sources of satisfaction; they have devoted considerable time to dating; and their friends are largely interested in dances and parties, as well. Not unexpectedly, these students report that they have spent less time than average studying and that they have read fewer books. They are less likely to expect to obtain higher degrees.

Political. Every campus has its politicians—those students who are leaders of the student government and who participate in various student clubs. Students who score high on this dimension report that they have been heavily involved in such activities, which provide important satisfactions of their college lives. Although they have read fewer books than average, they have spent an average amount of time studying, and they have average expectations for obtaining advanced degrees.

To some extent, of course, each student shares several of these orientations. There are few instances where a student's interests are confined to only one area. Table 1 shows that different dimensions of student interests and activities are related in expected ways. For example, those students who are involved in intellectual matters are somewhat likely to be involved also in activist (r = .34) and artistic (r = .43) endeavors. On the other hand, those students with their eyes fixed firmly on a vocational future are more likely to be academic (r = .40) and less likely to be part of the hip nonconformist culture (r = −.38).

These different orientations have their counterparts in the larger culture. The nation esteems men and women who excel in most of these areas; the citizenry admires its political and social leaders, its athletes and artists. Further, each of these different kinds of human activity has its attendant satisfactions. However, they are not equally appreciated by the academic culture. Most faculty members tend to value intellectual and academic activities; some support activist, vocational, and artistic activities; but most ignore or oppose the other four types of activities.

At first glance it may appear that some students have been

Table 1 Intercorrelations Between Student Orientations Toward College[a]

	Intellectual	Academic	Activist	Vocational	Artistic	Hip Noncon-formist	Athletic	Social	Political
Intellectual									
Academic	.06								
Activist	.34	−.16							
Vocational	−.12	.40	−.22						
Artistic	.43	−.09	.29	−.21					
Hip Nonconformist	.22	−.34	.40	−.38	.29				
Athletic	−.12	−.06	−.14	.18	−.19	−.11			
Social	−.09	−.02	.09	.22	−.03	−.06	.18		
Political	−.04	.14	.08	.28	−.04	−.15	.20	.38	

[a] $N = 1475$

interested in learning and some have not. But as will be shown, all have been learning. The point is that they have concentrated on learning different things, only some of which fit easily within a conventional academic framework.

Although students with these different kinds of interests are found in most schools and most majors, they are not randomly distributed. Rather, they are concentrated disproportionately in certain schools and in certain fields of study. In order to learn about their distributions, each dimension was divided into thirds, and the proportion of students scoring in the upper third was determined for each school and for each field of study. For example, 58 percent of the students in Raymond College, 53 percent in Stevenson College at Santa Cruz, and 48 percent in Monteith College scored high on the *intellectual* dimension. Each of these schools is relatively new, projects a strongly intellectual image, has innovative programs, and is a subunit of a larger university system—all factors that would attract and nurture intellectually oriented students. By contrast, only 15 percent of the students at Clark College, 22 percent at Luther College, and 24 percent at the College of the Pacific were in the top third of the *intellectual* dimension. These are all small denominational schools with more traditional and utilitarian programs that are less likely to attract or cultivate students with intrinsic intellectual interests.

In general, the three more experimental schools, as well as Shimer College, had a greater proportion of *hip nonconformist, artistic,* and *activist* students. The three more traditional schools, as well as Northeastern Illinois State College, had more *vocational, political, social,* and *athletic* students. The University of California at Berkeley, as might be expected of a multiversity, had something for everybody; no orientation was disproportionately found there.

Looking at fields of study, 47 percent of the students majoring in the humanities are in the top third of the *intellectual* scale while only 17 percent of those in education and 20 percent of those in other professional or applied fields of study are highly *intellectual.* Generally, the humanities tend to draw disproportionate numbers of *artistic* and *hip nonconformist* students, the natural sciences more *academic* and *athletic* students, the social sciences more *hip nonconformists,* education more *vocational, social,* and *political* students, and the other professional fields more *vocational* and *athletic* students. It should be obvious that these differential concentrations of students affect the character of teaching and learning found in each school and discipline.

Since these different kinds of student interests and activities are found on most campuses, one wonders how students with such different orientations to college life and to learning have coped with the academic side of college. More particularly: What kinds of relationships with teachers have they had? How have they changed during their college careers? And how satisfied are they with their college experiences? Answers to these questions may suggest ways to enhance both teaching and learning.

RELATIONSHIPS WITH FACULTY

There are many different levels on which a student may relate to a faculty member, both in and out of class, and several are explored here. Consider, first, classroom relationships. One important characteristic of faculty–student relationships in the classroom is the extent to which a student speaks out. Indeed, this is one of the primary ways in which teachers find out about the concerns of their students. One item on the senior questionnaire asked students to indicate how many times they had asked questions, volunteered answers, or made remarks in their most enjoyable courses of the most recent term.

Speaking out in class was most highly correlated with *intellectual, activist, artistic,* and *political* orientations. Since the first three of these dimensions represent intrinsic interests in ideas, it may be that students scoring high on these scales were more active participants largely because of their greater intellectual interests; students high on the *political* dimension may have participated because they are generally sociable persons. On the other hand, the *athletic* and *hip nonconformist* dimensions showed low correlation with participation in class. Among the "silent majority" of students are many whose interests are not primarily intellectual, and they are precisely the ones who are less likely to verbalize their interests to their teachers, even in their favorite courses.

Examination of student relationships with faculty members outside of class shows similar results. Students were asked to indicate the number of different conversations of ten minutes or more they had had with faculty members during the preceding month. Again *intellectual, activist,* and *artistic* orientations were most strongly related to such conversations, and *hip nonconformist* and *athletic* concerns were unrelated. Like classroom dialog, out-of-class discussions with students are important sources of information to faculty members, and this evidence suggests that faculty may obtain a biased sample of students from which to learn about their concerns.

Evidence for this interpretation that faculty obtain information about their students on a selective basis is the fact that out-of-class conversations tend to reflect the particular interests of students. For example, *intellectual* orientation was more highly related to conversations about academic or intellectual issues than to any other topic ($r = .31$); *vocational* orientation was most highly related to conversations concerning career plans or opportunities ($r = .24$); and *activist* orientation was most highly related to conversations about campus or social issues ($r = .35$).

The curriculum constitutes yet another level of faculty–student relationships. Some students are satisfied with the usual course offerings and teaching methods, while others prefer different ones. Those with higher *activist, intellectual, artistic* and *political* orientations are more likely to have helped initiate new courses, and they are also more likely to have taken independent study courses. On the other hand, students with high *athletic* orientation or high *vocational* orientation were least likely to have initiated alternative courses.

A persistent pattern emerges from these items: students who are most heavily involved in *intellectual, activist, artistic,* and (to a lesser extent) campus *political* activities have more actively cultivated relationships with faculty members than have students with other interests. On several levels they have been more aggressive and involved than students with other concerns—they have participated more in class, they have had more contact with faculty outside of class, and they have initiated more new or independent study courses. It is worth noting that students with high *academic* and *vocational* orientations, those who seem to study hardest, have taken a far more passive approach to faculty and courses. They appear to keep their distance from faculty, and seem to be more willing to play the game as given rather than to try to change the rules.

STUDENT GROWTH AND ACHIEVEMENT

Perhaps the most important question that can be asked of college seniors is what they have gained from their college experience. The questionnaire asked students to assess both their cognitive and affective change.

Cognitive growth was measured by an item asking students the degree of progress they have made toward several intellectual objectives. Virtually all students reported making at least some progress toward acquiring knowledge of specifics and knowledge of universals and abstractions in some field of study, toward developing the ability to comprehend or interpret communications, evaluate materials and methods, and apply principles to particular situations, and toward understanding scientific method. However, there was considerable variability between those who reported only some progress and those who reported much progress.

Students scoring high on the *intellectual* dimension said they made more progress in more areas than students scoring high on any of the other dimensions. They were higher than any of the other groups on learning abstractions, comprehending communications, and applying principles. Students scoring high on the *academic* and *vocational* dimensions, however, reported the most progress in learning the specifics of a field and in understanding scientific methods. This differential progress reflects the various cognitive styles of these three groups. The presence of all three of these distinct cognitive styles in a classroom would pose a challenge to any teacher.

Affective growth was assessed by asking seniors to indicate whether they decreased, changed little, or increased in a variety of personal attributes. Again, most students reported growth; for example, 86 percent of the total reported greater self-awareness, and 79 percent said they had developed more intellectual interests. But there was differential change reported by students with different involvements.

In general, more change was reported in those attributes consonant with the activities in which students had invested time and energy. That is, the greatest increase in general intellectual interests was reported by students with interests in the *intellectual* area ($r = .21$); the most increase in political awareness was reported by students involved in *activism* ($r = .22$); the largest increase in esthetic interests was reported by students with *artistic* orientation ($r = .39$); and the most improvement in emotional stability was reported by students with *social* ($r = .16$) and *vocational* ($r = .20$) orientation.

These self-reported changes are corroborated by measured changes on the Omnibus Personality Inventory (OPI). For example, the *intellectual* dimension was positively correlated not only with the senior OPI *Thinking Introversion* score, but also with the increase from freshman to senior years; the *artistic* dimension was positively correlated not only with the senior OPI *Estheticism* scale, but also with the amount of change from the freshman to senior years. Such findings confirm the self-reported affective changes of students on the senior questionnaire.

One other measure of achievement used was students' reported grade point averages. It should be no surprise to learn that grade point average was most highly related to *academic* ($r = .42$) and *intellectual* involvements ($r = .29$). On the other hand, grades were negatively related to concern with *social* ($r = -.17$), *athletic* ($r = -.12$), and *political* ($r = -.11$) activities. This finding suggests that just as there are different ways to make good grades so are there different ways to make poor grades. Heavy involvement in any of a number of extracurricular activities found on college campuses may have a deleterious effect on students' grade point averages.

In summary, more growth and achievement were reported by students on those attributes that are consistent with the activities in which they had invested time and energy.

SENIOR SATISFACTIONS AND FRESHMAN CHARACTERISTICS

Two more sets of data must be discussed before the various pieces of this analysis can be put together to show how students with these separate orientations have coped with the academic side of college. These data have to do with the degree to which seniors are satisfied with their college experiences and the characteristics of those same students when they entered college.

The overwhelming majority of seniors were satisfied with their college experience. Even though they had been on campus during the most turbulent educational era in memory, 77 percent said they were satisfied with their total college experience, 12 percent had neutral or mixed feelings, and only 10 percent were dissatisfied. This finding should not be too surprising, however, as the most dissatisfied students probably would not have persisted through four years at the same school.

More important for the purposes at hand are the sources of satisfaction among students with different orientations. The now-familiar pattern emerges once more: Students who have been more involved in a particular kind of activity are more satisfied with that aspect of college than are students who have been less involved. Of course, this would be true for those satisfactions that were used to help define the different dimensions—students with an *artistic* orientation deriving a great deal of personal satisfaction from artistic or literary work, those with an *athletic* orientation from athletics, those with a *social* orientation from parties and social life, those with a *political* orientation from student government, and so on. But it is true also for those items which are independent of the definers. Students with an *intellectual* orientation are most satisfied with independent study, those with *academic* and *vocational* orientations with traditional course work.

The discussion so far has focused on the senior questionnaire, and a single pattern has emerged in which students with different orientations have experienced differential relationships with faculty, growth, and satisfactions. It is relevant now to ask how far back that pattern is apparent. Did it develop before college or during college? To answer this question, responses to the OPI that these students gave when they were entering freshmen, can be examined.

There are two inferences to be drawn from this analysis. First, students high on each dimension were oriented in that direction even before they entered college. For example, even as freshmen students with an *intellectual* orientation were likely to score higher on the OPI scale *Thinking Introversion,* and those with an *artistic* orientation had higher scores on the *Estheticism* scale. Thus, even before students started college, their personal orientations provided an indication of which interests and activities they would pursue and which activities they would find most satisfying.

Second, each dimension is more highly correlated with the related senior personality scale than it is with the freshman scale. That is, students high on the *intellectual* dimension rank even higher on the *Thinking Introversion* scale of the OPI as seniors than they did as freshmen, and students high on the *artistic* dimension rank even higher on the *Esthetic* scale as seniors than as freshmen.

These findings—that students pursue activities in college that are consistent with their personal characteristics, and that those characteristics are accentuated as a result of their college experience—have been reported in several other studies (Astin & Panos, 1969; Feldman & Newcomb, 1969; Clark, et al., 1972). While college students generally change and develop in these areas from their freshman to senior years, it appears that the strongest individual gains occur in areas that are consistent with the strong interests these students had as freshmen.

ACCENTUATION OF INTERESTS

When these data are pieced together, they make a fairly clear picture. Students enter college with certain personal orientations; they get involved in activities consistent with those orientations; they develop relationships with faculty members in ways that grow out of their major concerns; they further develop cognitively and affectively in areas in which they have concentrated their attention; and they are satisfied with those aspects of college to which they have given themselves. In short, the qualities students bring to college generally tend to persist and become accentuated as a result of their college education.

These findings suggest a kind of museum model of education (as opposed to the traditional container model in which professors pour knowledge into the minds of students). In this museum model, students, when they enter college, are presented with many educational exhibits with which they may spend time. Depending upon their interests, students choose to spend time at certain exhibits and ignore or go quickly past others. Their experiences with certain objects whet their interests, sharpen their skills for understanding those objects, and give them expected satisfactions, while their interests and competencies concerning other artifacts languish. Colleges and universities, like museums, provide displays for everyone, even those who are not interested in the main presentations and perhaps would rather not have come in the first place. Only the most provocative and stimulating exhibits are able to capture the attention of those not already interested in them.

This conclusion is based on averages of all the students' experiences; such an analysis may provide a general picture but it masks many individual differences. Some students have undoubtedly changed directions in college, and some have undoubtedly been dissatisfied with what they have experienced. Variations will be explored in the following chapters, but the overall trend is already apparent.

Chapter 12

Significant Faculty–Student Relationships

Institutions of higher learning, like any of society's institutions, will never have enough personable, dynamic, and magnetic staff or bright, highly motivated, self-confident clients, no matter how diligently they attempt to recruit them. Such persons are in relatively short supply. Effective college teaching and learning, however, depend not only on the personal qualities of faculty and students but also on the nature of the relationships by which they are joined. Since interpersonal relationships are heavily influenced by institutional arrangements, substantial improvement in education might be achieved by creating conditions that maximize the likelihood of significant encounters occurring between greater numbers of teachers and students.

This chapter will focus on the nature of particularly significant relationships as seen by both faculty members and students. The following research questions are addressed:

- From the faculty perspective, what are some of the key characteristics of their fruitful relationships with students?
- Where faculty feel that they have made different kinds of contributions to students' development, what aspects of the relationships, such as intimacy and duration, are related to these different types of contributions?
- From the student perspective, what are the key characteristics of their relationships with faculty members who contribute most to their development?

- Where students report different kinds of faculty influence, what kinds of relationships are associated with each?
- What are the similarities and differences between faculty and student perceptions?

THE FACULTY VIEW

Since the data used to answer these questions are the self-reports of faculty and students, an effort was made to make them as reliable as possible by asking respondents about specific relationships. Each faculty member was asked to name a senior to whose personal or educational development he had contributed a great deal, to describe the relationship, and to indicate the extent to which he had helped that student in several areas. Of the 590 faculty members who had taught seniors, 407—69 percent—named such students and completed this portion of the questionnaire.

Most of the faculty members said they had known the students they named for some substantial proportion of the students' college careers. Only 17 percent said they had first come to know the students when they were seniors; 34 percent said they had come to know the students as juniors, 25 percent as sophomores, and 22 percent as freshmen. Apparently the perception of having had an impact—at least of the greatest impact—is generally dependent on a faculty member's having experienced a *continuing* relationship with a student over a substantial period of time.

Continuity of interaction between a faculty member and a student throughout the student's educational career is amenable to administrative manipulations in a number of ways. The assigning of educational advisors is one such device. There is some evidence that this is an effective practice, because faculty were formally assigned as advisors to the students they named in 25 percent of the cases. While this finding may mean that advisors exert influence on the educational and/or personal development of students, it may also reflect the fact that students choose as advisors faculty members who previously have influenced them or who are people the students judge to be capable of helping them.

Courses, too, seem to be a relatively potent device for creating the kind of continuity that leads to perceived impact on the part of faculty members. A large minority of faculty—44 percent—said that the students they named had taken three or more courses with them. Another 53 percent said that the students had taken one or two of their courses; only three percent of the faculty said that the students had taken no courses with them. One of the effects of courses on faculty–student relationships is that they engender acceptance of responsibilities by each party; that is, a faculty member tends to conceive of the students in his courses as *his* students and to feel a greater responsibility to them than to other students, and students who have been helped to an unusual degree by a teacher are likely to elect to take courses that he offers. This acceptance of responsibilities explains why virtually all students named had taken at least one and usually several courses with the faculty members.

When asked to describe the relationships they had with the students named, most faculty characterized them as "casual and friendly." This response was chosen by 72 percent of the faculty, whereas only six percent said the relationships were "impersonal," and 22 percent said they were "close and personal." Given the special character of the relationship specified and the freedom the faculty had to name any students on whom they had exerted significant influence, it is perhaps surprising that more did not regard the relationship as close and personal. Yet the fact that a single teacher may be teaching dozens and perhaps hundreds of students at any one time may make it impossible for him to develop personal relationships with very many students. And other research (Gamson, 1967) has shown that many faculty hold a democratic view and strive to express

Table 1　Frequency of Faculty Discussion of Selected Topics with Nominated Students, in percentages[a]

Topics	Never (1)	Rarely (2)	Sometimes (3)	Often (4)	Total
Educational plans	1	4	35	60	100
Course work in general	1	7	33	59	100
Specific academic projects	0	8	34	57	99
Career plans	2	7	36	56	101
Values and personal philosophy	6	20	42	33	101
Personal problems or concerns	10	20	43	26	99
Social and political issues	11	26	39	24	100
Campus controversies	15	25	40	20	100

[a] N = 407

[b] Total percentages vary because all percentages were rounded to nearest whole numbers

Table 2   Extent to which Faculty Perceive that They Have Influenced Nominated Students, in percentages[a]

Area of Influence	Not at all as far as I know	To some extent	To a great extent
Formulation of career plans	22	53	25
Decisions about a major field of study	27	49	25
Acquiring an appreciation of the values and methods of inquiry	12	66	22
Developing a personal philosophy or outlook on life	30	61	9

[a] $N = 407$

equal concern for all students, a stance that may prevent them from becoming especially close to any one student.

While significant relationships are heavily concerned with academic issues—and indeed such issues seem to form a basis for such impactful relationships—most involve a wide range of discussions, implying a concern for and involvement of the whole student, if not the whole teacher. The frequencies with which faculty said they talked with students about a variety of topics are shown in Table 1. The topics most often discussed are those directly related to faculty roles, such as course work in general, educational plans, specific academic projects, and career plans. However, between one-third and one-fifth of the faculty said that they often discussed topics less closely related to traditional teaching roles, such as values and personal philosophy, personal problems or concerns, social and political issues, and campus controversies; very few (6 to 15 percent) said that they never discussed these topics with the students they nominated.

Faculty also were asked to indicate whether they thought they were helpful or influential in each of several areas. As Table 2 shows, a large majority thought that they had been helpful, at least to some extent, in each of the four areas specified. Furthermore, between 21 and 25 percent said that they had been influential "to a great extent" in regard to the formulation of career plans, decisions about a major field of study, and acquiring an appreciation of the values and methods of inquiry. For at least those students they nominated, students with whom they enjoyed a long-term, broadly based relationship, faculty felt that they had exerted influence in a number of areas.

Are particular aspects of significant relationships related to the *type* of contribution faculty perceive they make to the lives of nominated students? In order to answer this question, various faculty-perceived contributions were correlated with each other and with aspects of the relationships. The intercorrelations among the four influence items yielded three useful findings. First, helping a student acquire an appreciation of scholarly inquiry was positively correlated with each of the other areas ($r = .32$ with deciding on a major, $r = .30$ with formulating career plans, and $r = .23$ with developing a personal philosophy), suggesting that intellectual influence may mediate all of the other areas of influence from the point of view of faculty members. Second, major and career planning were highly correlated ($r = .68$), indicating the close relationship not only between a student's future career and his educational planning, but also between a faculty member's interest and ability to give advice in the two areas. And third, contributing to a student's outlook on life was negligibly related to giving assistance with both major ($r = .14$) and career ($r = .13$) plans. Apparently, affecting a student's personal philosophy is not substantially related to affecting his educational or vocational plans.

If this is so, it may be useful to ask whether affecting a student's personal outlook grows out of a different kind of relationship than helping him to make career plans. In order to answer this question, faculty responses about the extent to which they were influential in the nominated students' development of personal philosophies on the one hand and formulation of career plans on the other were correlated with responses about other aspects of these particularly potent relationships.

Those who perceived they had helped students in both ways had discussed different issues with students. In the correlations of these faculty perceptions, having had a personal impact on the students nominated was positively related to having talked about values and personal philosophy ($r = .45$), personal problems or concerns ($r = .28$), social and political issues ($r = .28$), and campus controversies ($r = .20$). These are all topics with implications for a student's personal philosophy, and it is understandable that faculty who discuss these things help students to develop their outlooks on life. But personal impact was unrelated to discussion about the students' careers ($r = .09$) or educational plans ($r = .14$).

On the other hand, playing a large role in helping the nominated students formulate their career plans was related, predictably, to the amount of discussion of their career plans ($r = .48$) and their educational plans ($r = .43$); it was only negligibly related to discussing personal issues ($r = .02$), campus controversies ($r = .03$), and social issues ($r = .10$).

Other aspects of these especially potent faculty–student relationships varied with the nature of the contributions faculty made to students. Perceiving impact on the nominated students' outlooks on life was positively associated with the total amount of discussion over all the areas listed in the questionnaire ($r = .53$) and with the closeness of the relationships ($r = .25$). The amount and closeness of interaction are both factors that would enhance the potency of a relationship and increase the likelihood that a faculty member would both affect something so central to a student as his outlook on life and perceive the effect. Neither of the factors, however, is as essential for influencing career decisions, or at least for a faculty member's perception of that contribution, as both of these measures are less strongly related to that kind of assistance.

Thus, from the point of view of faculty members, there is a special quality in their relationships with students to whose educational and/or personal development they feel they have contributed a great deal. These relationships are characterized by a continuity of interaction, by casual and friendly attitudes, by extensive and wide-ranging discussions, and by a high degree of intellectuality. In addition, the amount and closeness of interaction are particularly related to faculty perceptions of having impact on the students' outlooks on life.

THE STUDENT VIEW

To obtain the other side of the picture, each student was asked to name the particular faculty member who had contributed the most to his educational and/or personal development. A total of 1127— or 77 percent—of the seniors named such faculty members. Most of the remaining students in the survey left the item blank, but a few of them wrote in colorful comments—for example, "No such animal"— indicating that they believed strongly that no faculty members had played significant roles in their development. Whether or not the same faculty–student relationships were being described by the faculty and students, the two groups tended to describe these particularly significant relationships in similar ways.

Like the faculty, students implied that the relationships had a good deal of continuity. Sixty-five percent of the students had taken two or more courses from the faculty members they nominated. This finding may mean that students tend to choose courses offered by faculty from whom they have profited, but it may also mean that taking several courses from a single faculty member provides an opportunity for truly significant relationships to form. Students are likely to take their concerns and problems to faculty members whom they know and feel they are known by; teachers encountered in a number of courses tend to fit that description.

Most students said that their interaction with the nominated faculty members extended beyond the classroom. Although 24 percent said they had never or seldom had contact outside of class with the faculty members, the majority had gone beyond the usual classroom relationship. Forty-five percent said they had talked with the faculty members outside of class occasionally, 19 percent said quite often, and another 12 percent said frequently. Thus, while a few of these especially impactful faculty members made their contributions without seeing the students outside of class, such instances were relatively rare.

Students were also asked to indicate the ways in which the nominated faculty members had helped them. Ten ways were stated, and the students were asked to indicate how descriptive each statement was for the faculty members nominated. As can be seen in Table 3, the statement gaining the highest degree of subscription, "was available and open to any discussion," was called very descriptive by 51 percent, with another 30 percent calling it quite descriptive. The key role of accessibility of faculty in facilitating interaction with students is discussed in Chapter 14, but here it is important to note that openness and availability of faculty members are the most important aspects of the most significant relationships that students have formed with faculty.

Another key characteristic of these influential relationships is the degree of intellectual stimulation involved. A total of 81 percent of the students said that the faculty members named stimulated them intellectually, and 66 percent said that the faculty members had interested them in their fields. Whatever else the relationships did for the students, they helped turn the students on to new ideas. Other statements said to be descriptive of the ways the faculty members helped the students were "helped me feel confident of my own

Table 3 Student Perceptions of the Ways Influential Faculty Members Helped Them, in percentages

Statement	Not at All Descriptive (1)	Somewhat Descriptive (2)	Quite Descriptive (3)	Very Descriptive (4)
He or she:				
was available and open to any discussion	4	14	30	51
stimulated me intellectually	3	16	35	46
helped me feelconfident of my own abilities	9	18	35	37
demanded high quality work from me	11	19	32	37
interested me in his/her field	10	24	31	35
encouraged me to inspect my values	31	25	26	17
advised me about my career plans	31	31	22	16
made me aware of social issues	36	31	21	13
counseled me about a personal problem	59	22	9	10
helped me get a job or scholarship	71	12	8	10

abilities" and "demanded high quality work from me." Pushing students to high but attainable levels of achievement is a delicate process but one that, if successful, may generate self-confidence in students. The evidence suggests that the teachers regarded by students as having contributed most to them were effective in matching their academic expectations with the students' abilities.

How are the different kinds of contributions students received from the nominated faculty members related to one another and to different aspects of the relationships? In order to answer this question the responses to three statements indicative of intellectual stimulation ("stimulated me intellectually," "interested me in his/her field," and "demanded high quality work from me") were summed, as were the two statements concerning value influence ("made me aware of social issues" and "encouraged me to inspect my values") and the statements reflecting career assistance ("advised me about my career plans" and "helped me get a job or scholarship"). Correlation coefficients between these three kinds of contributions were then computed.

Being stimulated intellectually showed low positive correlations with experiencing value development and obtaining assistance in career planning ($r = .25$ and $r = .22$, respectively). These positive correlations suggest that both having one's values challenged and receiving assistance in one's career are associated with, and perhaps mediated by, intellectually stimulating relationships. The correlation between the summed score of the two items descriptive of value development and the summed score of the two items descriptive of career assistance is negligible, however, ($r = -.04$), suggesting that these are relatively independent kinds of influence.

Additional analyses revealed that different aspects of these relationships were associated with different kinds of help students reported. Receiving career assistance from these faculty members seems particularly to be an outcome of having formed close and continuous relationships with those teachers both in class and out of class. The number of courses taken with the nominated faculty members was positively correlated with career assistance ($r = .23$), and the amount of interaction with teachers outside of class was positively correlated with career contributions ($r = .45$). From the student perspective, obtaining advice about a career, especially help in obtaining a job or scholarship, is a more individual task that must of necessity take place in out-of-class discussions between faculty and students.

SIMILARITIES IN VIEWPOINTS

Although they were not necessarily looking at the same relationships, both faculty and students described particularly impactful relationships as unusually close and continuous. Such relationships were unlikely to occur unless faculty and students were brought together in at least one course, and they were more commonly the result of being associated in two or more courses. Yet, in most cases, the relationships that made a difference in the lives of students extended beyond the classroom. Furthermore, both faculty and students reported that such relationships were characterized by a good deal of intellectual excitement—a finding of such import that the factors involved in facilitating the intellectual development of students are examined in more detail in Chapter 13.

The amount, duration, and closeness of interaction with students were particularly associated with the perception among faculty of having helped students develop personal philosophies or outlooks on life. It has been suggested that this may be because only in such relationships can faculty learn that they have affected students' values. Another interpretation may be that faculty tended to nominate students whose values they think they have affected because they, as well as their students, are touched by discussions of social and personal values. For some faculty members, talking about social issues with reference to students' value schemes may be a welcome change from the relationships they may consider more mundane, such as providing advice about what career opportunities exist for students majoring in a particular field. Indeed, such discussions may have personal implications for the faculty members' own value schemes. Faculty may thus have focused upon what is rare and personally relevant to them in describing the students they nominated.

Among students, the amount, duration, and closeness of interaction with the teachers who were perceived to have contributed the most to their development were more strongly associated with receiving assistance in their careers than with other kinds of faculty influence. Such aid acquires a personal tone, especially to seniors who are preparing to graduate from college. Although some professors may believe that students can improve the quality of their lives by inspecting their values rather than preparing for careers, students know that the kind of work they choose to enter will profoundly affect the quality of their personal lives. In addition, since obtaining guidance about career alternatives requires some individual contact outside of class, it may have been seen by students to be the result of close interpersonal relationships with faculty members.

Despite the fact that faculty and students perceived that the amount and kind of interaction was differentially associated with different kinds of influence, the general conclusion seems to be that both students and faculty hold pictures of salient faculty–student relationships that are strikingly similar.

Chapter 13

Facilitating
Intellectual Development

Although most faculty members perceived that they helped students acquire an appreciation for the values and methods of scholarly inquiry, and although most students said that they were stimulated intellectually, a nagging question persists. Did the students *really* change intellectually? Often implicit in questions like this is a conception of intellectual change that stresses the acquisition of facts, theories, and methods of a field of study.

A different and somewhat broader conception stresses the development of interest in ideas and the personal openness to pursue them. This view of intellect is concerned not with the acquisition of a specific body of knowledge which may soon become dated, but rather with the development of a positive attitude toward ideas which may help the student continue learning long after he leaves college. This second view is consistent with the tradition of liberal education enshrined in statements of purpose in most college catalogs, such as the following from the catalog of one of the schools in this study:

> This college believes in an education which not only trains young minds and fills them with knowledge, but opens them and makes them flexible and resilient enough to grow and to meet the challenge of accelerated change which will confront them throughout their lives.

Such a proclamation of the liberal education creed could have appeared in virtually any college catalog in the country. But how many students actually become more interested in ideas, as well as open, flexible, and resilient? Why is it that some students are affected this way by college while others are not? What kinds of teaching facilitates such intellectual and personal development? The first part of this chapter attempts to shed light on these questions by comparing the college experiences of students who have actually become more open, intellectually and personally, with those of students who have not evidenced such change. The second part examines the kinds of teachers and teaching that students who have changed credit with having contributed most to their development.

The degree of intellectual change was measured by the Omnibus Personality Inventory (OPI), a personality test that has been widely used to study changes in college students. The theoretical and empirical character of the OPI makes it an appropriate measure of the sort of intellectual growth liberal arts programs presume to foster. It contains measures of four different kinds of intellectual interests: the *Thinking Introversion* scale measures interest in a broad range of ideas and in reflective thought; the *Theoretical Orientation* scale indicates interest in logical, abstract, and scientific thinking; the *Estheticism* scale reflects artistic and literary interests; and the *Complexity* scale indicates preference for a flexible, open approach to problems. Because Heist and Yonge (1968), the authors of the OPI, theorized that "a readiness or freedom to deal with ideas and new cognitive experiences" would be necessary to allow students to pursue the interests measured by these scales, they added scales of *Autonomy,* assessing independence of judgment, and *Religious Orientation,* indicating freedom from fundamentalist constraints.

Using a student's score on each of these six scales, Heist and Yonge have developed a formula that assigns him to one of eight Intellectual Disposition Categories (IDC). These categories are:

- *Category One* Broad intrinsic interests with strong literary and esthetic perspectives.
- *Category Two* Intrinsic interests oriented toward dealing with concepts and abstractions.
- *Category Three* Intellectuality emphasizing problem-solving and rational thinking.
- *Category Four* Intellectuality tempered by an achievement orientation and a disciplinary focus.
- *Category Five* Interest in academic matters and achievement, but as a means toward an end.
- *Category Six* Attenuated learning orientation with vocational and practical emphases.

- *Category Seven*   Nonintellectual with no interest in ideas or literary and esthetic matters.
- *Category Eight*   Anti-intellectual, but not uninterested in tangibles and learning the practical.

This scheme permits classification along a continuum that ranges from students with broad, intrinsic intellectual interests and personal qualities of openness and flexibility to those students with restricted, pragmatic, and even nonintellectual concerns and closed and inflexible personalities. If a student were receiving the expected benefits of a liberal education, he presumably would develop more intellectual interests and greater personal freedom, which would be reflected in his increase in intellectual disposition over his four years of college study.

For several reasons it was decided to focus this analysis on those students who entered college with moderate intellectual dispositions—those in Categories Four, Five, or Six. First, this middle range is where the largest proportion of students is found; 1033 of the students in this sample had freshman IDC scores in this range. Second, focusing upon this group allows one to avoid some technical measurement problems, such as ceiling and floor effects, that are inherent in extreme scores. Third, it has been found in previous research (Clark, et. al., 1972) that IDC changes are more likely to occur among students who enter with moderate scores.

Among this group a total of 484 students increased one or more categories, while 549 remained in the same category or fell to a lower one. This finding is consistent with other research (Clark, et. al., 1972, p. 156) that found that in several diverse schools approximately half of the students increased in intellectual disposition. Although *average* gains by groups of college students on a *single trait* are quite common—as seen in Chapter 11 and in previous research (Feldman & Newcomb, 1969)—the averages mask the fact that some *individuals* change in terms of a *profile* of intellectual interests and personality characteristics, while others do not. According to these data, fewer than half of the students became sufficiently more interested in a broad range of ideas and became more personally open during the four years they spent in college to increase even one step in the intellectual disposition scale.

In order to learn more about the students who evidence this kind of growth and those who do not, freshman and senior questionnaire responses were examined for the two groups of students: the change group (those who increased one or more intellectual categories) and the nonchange group (those who either failed to change or decreased in intellectual disposition). As will be shown, a distinctive configuration of orientations to college, interactions with faculty, satisfactions, and conceptions of an ideal college differentiated the change group from the nonchange group.

One of the first things that became apparent is that seniors who increased in intellectual disposition also had the subjective feeling of having changed more. The change group reported more cognitive progress than the nonchange group, particularly in mastering universals and abstractions in some field of study and in developing the abilities to comprehend or interpret ideas, to evaluate materials and methods of study, and to apply abstractions of principles to particular situations. Apparently this finding is not simply an artifact of these students' generally optimistic assessment of their educational progress, because they did not, to a statistically significant extent, say that they also had learned more about the specifics of a field, such as terminology, or about the scientific method. Rather, their assessment is that they have made much progress in developing the higher level intellectual skills of learning to generalize, comprehend, evaluate, and apply ideas; but they do not differ from students in the non-change group in acquiring more factual details or greater under-standing of scientific method.

Although most seniors said that they had undergone a variety of af-fective changes, those who increased one or more categories in in-tellectual disposition had the subjective feeling of having changed more in these characteristics. When compared with the nonchange group, more of them reported increasing self-awareness, intellectual interests in general, political concerns or awareness, concern with social issues, and scope and awareness of ethical standards. More of them also reported becoming more liberal; they had increased in both political liberalness and acceptance of other racial groups. In short, those students who have been designated as the change group by virtue of their OPI profile shifts perceive that they have changed in ways that may be summarized as greater intellectual growth, personal openness, and social awareness—changes consonant with the liberal arts ideal.

Why do some students change intellectually? Or, perhaps it is more to the point to ask why some do not change, especially when they are in one of the more malleable stages of their lives and have lived four years in a setting ostensibly designed to produce change. One possi-bility is that the change and nonchange groups were different in some important ways when they entered college. This possibility was explored by examining their responses to certain items on the freshman questionnaire. The groups differed statistically on only two out of 66 comparisons, a result likely to be obtained by chance alone. As freshmen, they did not differ in their educational goals, curricular philosophy (required courses versus student freedom to choose courses), views of the importance of grades, degree of interest in various activities (including intellectual, political, and financial matters), reasons for selecting their colleges (including general academic reputation, variety of elective courses, and strength of particular departments), how much they knew about several features of the schools they were about to enter (including the general philosophies of the colleges, the variety of course offerings, and the extent of informal faculty–student contact), and the satisfactions they expected to derive from several aspects of college life (including course work, individual study, and getting acquainted with faculty members). These results indicate that neither intellectual change nor lack of intellectual change can be attributed to any of these factors which the students brought with them to college.

CORRELATES OF CHANGE

As seniors, however, students in the change group reported a distinctive configuration of orientations toward college, interactions with faculty, satisfactions, and conceptions of an ideal college. In considering these correlates, a few of the major events that occurred between 1966 and 1970, the time when these students were in college, should be kept in mind. The rise of New Left thinking, trenchant criticism of virtually all social institutions, including colleges and universities themselves, and a myriad of proposals for the creation of alternative institutions were among the major intellectual developments. The campuses became centers of direct political action with large numbers of students attending rallies, picketing, marching, and otherwise working for or against certain causes. Artistic and literary productions grew more boldly explicit and strikingly powerful with the advent of new visual and audio media. Nonconformist countercultures, complete with underground newspapers and an array of hallucinogenic drugs, became widespread among youth. The data indicate that students who became more intellectually disposed were more involved in each of these several kinds of developments than those who did not change.

Analyzed in terms of scales of student interests and activities (see Chapter 11), students in the change group were more likely to have been involved in *artistic, intellectual, activist,* and *hip nonconformist* activities. As can be seen in Table 1, increase in IDC was positively correlated with each of these scales.

It is interesting to observe that, on the average, students in the change group did not engage in *social, athletic,* and *political* activities any more or any less than students in the nonchange group. It is also instructive to note that *vocational* and *academic* students, those whose activities include the greatest academic involvement (hours studying) and academic achievement (grades), were least likely to increase in IDC. They appear to have focused so narrowly on instrumental academic activities that they did not expand their intellectual interests and adopted such a dependent relationship to their teachers that they did not develop personal autonomy. It would seem that, for students in the change group, taking part in the controversial events of the 1960s—not keeping their noses to the academic grindstone nor concentrating on preparation for careers—was instrumental in fostering intellectual and personal development. And ironically, this was happening while many college faculty members and administrative authorities were growing increasingly concerned about the harm these developments were causing to education on their campuses.

Table 1   Correlations Between Change in Intellectual Disposition and Student Orientations to College as Seniors

Student Orientation	Correlation with Increase in Intellectual Disposition[a]
Artistic	.36
Intellectual	.32
Activist	.31
Hip Nonconformist	.22
Political	.06
Athletic	.04
Social	.00
Academic	−.09
Vocational	−.12

[a] A correlation of .08 is significant at the .01 level

One motivation underlying student involvement in these activities appears to be an attempt to develop self-awareness. This inference is supported by answers to another question. When asked about the importance of developing or expanding their self-awareness, 66 percent of the students in the change group said that it was of extreme importance, a response given by only 43 percent of the students in the nonchange group. More students in the change group seem to have sought out experiences that were intellectually and personally stimulating to them.

In addition, students in the change group seem to have been more aggressive in seeking out faculty members to pursue their interests. This aggressiveness may be seen in two different areas—in their more frequent interaction with faculty outside of class and in their more frequent initiation of independent study courses. More students in the change group had frequent out-of-class discussions with faculty concerning campus or social issues and academic or intellectual issues. Since it is usually the students who initiate out-of-class conversations with faculty, they seem to have exercised the initiative to seek out experiences that would be related to their interests. And 58 percent of the students in the change group, compared with 43 percent of the students in the nonchange group, had taken independent study courses. Bess and Bilorusky (1970) have found that student-initiated courses characteristically tend to be concerned with topics not found in the usual curriculum (such as contemporary social problems, community activity, and affective experiences), that students who initiate them tend to be more autonomous and independent, and that the students deliberately attempt to structure a portion of their college environment so that it is responsive to their interests. Taken together, these findings suggest that students who become more intellectually disposed more aggressively utilize both faculty members and curricular alternatives to enhance their own self-awareness.

There are differences in the degree to which student aggressiveness is associated with IDC change in different institutions. Because the sample was heavily weighted by students from the Berkeley campus, separate analyses of the correlates of change were performed for students there and for those in the rest of the institutions. The amount of contact with faculty discussing both intellectual and social issues was more highly associated with increase in IDC at Berkeley than in the other schools. This suggests that students in the change group at this large school, which has not been regarded as being particularly hospitable to undergraduates, had to be more aggressive than those at the smaller schools in seeking out stimulating discussions with faculty. With this exception, the correlates of IDC change discussed here are generally similar at Berkeley and at the other schools.

Another concomitant of whether a student changed or not was his major field of study. While students in the change group were located in all fields, more of them had majored in the humanities and fewer had concentrated in mathematics and the natural sciences. Thirty-five percent of the students in the change group majored in the humanities, compared with 15 percent in mathematics and the natural sciences; among the students in the nonchange group, the comparable percentages were 28 and 21. Although some critics (Arrowsmith, 1967; Kampf, 1967) had asserted that at the time of this study the humanities had turned away from considering human issues, the content of these fields, more than most, would tend to satisfy a student's need to analyze himself. Furthermore, fields such as literature and philosophy are somewhat less rigidly codified than chemistry and physics (see Chapter 6), a condition that would offer the student the latitude he seeks to explore issues of current interest.

In this vein, another finding concerning the special impact of certain kinds of literature may be mentioned. Students were asked to indicate the most significant influences (events, persons, literature, etc.) on their thinking and life during the college years. Although there were no differences between the groups on most influences, 31 percent of the students who changed volunteered the name of some book or author who had been popular on the campuses. Books such as *Stranger in a Strange Land* and *Autobiography of Malcolm X*, novelists such as Hesse and Vonnegut, philosophers such as Marcuse and Camus, and psychologists such as Freud and Perls were mentioned as having been the most significant influences in the lives of 152—31 percent—of the students in the change group. This kind of literature, with many personal and social reference points, was named important by only 16 percent of the students in the nonchange group. Such reading is more likely to be encountered in courses in the humanities than in other fields. It is also noteworthy that textbooks were seldom included in the category of influential literature.

In addition to this direct evidence of the kinds of college experiences associated with increase in intellectual disposition, two pieces of indirect evidence may be considered. Since people generally tend to do those things they find satisfying (see Chapter 11), a clue to the experiences of students may be found in their satisfactions. Fifty-three percent of the students in the change group said that individual study or research had been an important source of satisfaction, compared with 41 percent of the students in the non-change group, and 31 percent of the students in the change group said that getting to know faculty members was important, compared with 24 percent of the students in the nonchange group. These two factors are probably interrelated. When a student does individual research, he often works closely with a faculty member whom he gets to know better; conversely, if a student gets acquainted with a faculty member, that teacher may be more likely to support his independent work. Students in the change group also found self-discovery and self-insight, individual artistic or literary work, bull sessions with fellow students, and political activism to have been more important sources of satisfaction than students in the nonchange group. The students who changed may have used their individualized study, artistic work, and political activities as avenues of self-exploration. Their conversations with peers and faculty members may well have been used to conceptualize and assimilate these experiences.

As another bit of indirect evidence of different experiences, it is interesting to note the kind of features students in the change group said they would build into their ideal colleges. They scored higher on a scale that contained such items as "working closely with teachers," "much emphasis on independent study," "mostly group discussion classes or seminars," and "closely knit college community." More of the students in the change group also would have their ideal schools place emphasis on broad, general programs rather than on specialized areas, and they would have courses graded "pass" or "fail" rather than with letter grades. It should not be thought, however, that this utopia is devoid of intellectual content: Sixty-three percent of the students in the change group, as opposed to 51 percent of the students in the nonchange group, would prefer to have a highly rigorous academic program. Their ideal could be characterized as a close intellectual community—an ideal strikingly similar to the classic conception of the liberal arts ideal. Although it is not possible to know for certain whether this ideal grew out of experiences within an intellectual community or whether it represents a craving for a kind of education they were denied, it seems to have been the result of their college experiences, because as freshmen the two groups did not hold different views of the ideal college.

There is some evidence that colleges have in certain ways failed to live up to the expectations of the students in the change group. It has already been shown that these students have taken more independent study courses, a fact that implies a certain dissatisfaction with the usual course offerings. But more, only 35 percent of the total (there being no significant difference between the two groups) said that course work in general was an important source of satisfaction, while 73 percent of the total said that course work in their fields of major interest was important. It would seem that the students in the change group are more likely to be turned off by traditional course-lecture-exam fare and that this may have provided some of the impetus for them to be more aggressive in initiating independent study courses and in pursuing informal, out-of-class discussions with faculty members. It is there, more than within the traditional academic offerings, that they may concentrate on those things that matter most to them. Of course, the greater satisfaction students derive from course work in their major is understandable, for such courses usually deal with issues in which they are most interested, and most faculty members have greater enthusiasm for teaching courses for their major students. In many schools, not all large, the closest approximation to an intellectual community may be found in certain departments where several faculty members and upper division students majoring in that field engage in dialog in small seminars, laboratories, or faculty offices. Such opportunities are less often available to students in survey, general education, or service courses.

A fairly clear pattern has emerged to differentiate the experiences of students who grew intellectually and personally open from those who failed to make such growth. Students in the change group appear to have made special efforts to expand their self-awareness. To a greater extent than those students who did not change, they became involved in a wide range of intellectual, artistic, activist, and hip nonconformist activities; they sought out faculty members for discussions of intellectual and social and campus issues; they tended to concentrate in the humanities; and they read a type of influential humanistic literature with strong personal and social overtones. In addition, they obtained greater satisfaction from many of these activities, and they developed an ideal of a college or university as an intellectual community.

THE MORE . . . THE MORE

Since the students who became more intellectually disposed had experiences that differed from their peers who did not, one wonders whether students who changed more had more of those experiences than those who changed a smaller amount. Among the students who changed, 305 increased one Intellectual Disposition Category, and 179 gained two or more. These two groups, as well as the nonchange group, were compared on each of the variables previously discussed. The general result is that the *degree* of change—in addition to the *existence* of change—is positively related to virtually all of these same variables. That is, the more students increased in Intellectual Disposition Categories, the more they were likely to have had the kinds of experiences that differentiated the change group from the nonchange group. For example, 43 percent of the students in the nonchange group had taken individual study courses, compared with 54 percent of the students who increased one IDC and 65 percent of the students who increased two or more IDCs.

This trend may be seen more clearly in Table 2. Individual study or research was said to have been important to their personal satisfaction by 41 percent of the students who showed no growth, by 47 percent of those who increased one IDC, and by 63 percent of those who increased two or more IDCs. The same pattern holds for the other items. Thus, not only have the students in the change group said that individual study, getting to know teachers, self-discovery, individual artistic work, bull sessions, and political activism have been more important to them than to the students in the nonchange group, but these activities have been even more important to those who changed the most.

Table 2 Students Who Said that Selected Activities Were Important for Their Personal Satisfaction, in percentages

Activities	Nonchange (N = 549)	One IDC Increase (N = 305)	Two or More IDCs Increase (N = 179)
Individual study or research	41	47	63
Getting to know faculty members	24	26	39
Self-discovery, self-insight	69	83	89
Individual artistic or literary work	20	28	45
Bull sessions with fellow students	48	58	64
Political activism	6	7	14

TEACHERS WHO WERE INTELLECTUALLY INFLUENTIAL

What kind of teaching was found helpful by the students who became more intellectually oriented? While it would be possible to make some rather sophisticated inferences purely on the basis of the kinds of experiences and influences that students in the change group reported, the study design has made it possible to obtain more direct evidence concerning this question. As already noted, students were asked to describe the faculty members whom they felt had contributed most to their educational or personal development. One set of descriptive statements about these faculty members was used to form a scale of *Intellectual Stimulation* along which the nominated faculty varied. Teachers scoring high on this dimension were said by students to have stimulated them intellectually, to have demanded high quality work from them, to have helped them feel confident of their own abilities, to have been available and open to any discussion, and to have interested them in the teachers' fields. Intellectually influential faculty members were defined as those designated as having contributed the most to the development of the students and who scored in the upper two-thirds of the *Intellectual Stimulation* scale.

A total of 46 faculty were nominated and described as having generated intellectual stimulation by two or more students who increased two or more steps on the IDC scale. The questionnaire responses of this group of 46 faculty members were compared with those of the remaining 756 faculty members to learn how they made their intellectual contributions to the students who changed the most. This group constitutes a substantial subset of the sample of student-nominated effective teachers already discussed in Chapter 10, and as will become apparent, the intellectually influential faculty resembled the generally effective teachers previously described.

More of the faculty said to have been intellectually influential were interested in undergraduate teaching. When asked to indicate their preferences among alternative activities, 79 percent of the nominated faculty selected teaching undergraduate students over teaching graduate students. Sixty-four percent of the comparison group preferred the undergraduate level.

Faculty were asked to indicate how often they engaged in certain classroom teaching behaviors, and it was hypothesized that the influential ones might behave differently than their colleagues. This proposition was tested by comparing the scores of the two groups on four classroom teaching scales. The influential faculty differed on only one of the scales, *Presentation Interest.* This measure was composed of items such as relating the course content to current social problems, using examples from their own experience or research, and trying to present materials in an entertaining way. These activities are indicative of an effort to enliven the course content, to make it connect with events and realities outside the class, and thereby to stimulate students intellectually. Thirty-seven percent of the influential faculty scored high on this scale, compared with 27 percent of their colleagues; 13 percent scored low, as did 38 percent of the comparison group.

It is perhaps as interesting to note that the two groups were indistinguishable on the three other classroom teaching scales, *Student Participation, Discursiveness,* and *Teaching Organization.* The dominant impression left by these data is that however faculty go about their teaching—whether they involve students in classroom activities, conduct wide-ranging, discursive intellectual analyses, or make well-organized presentations—intellectual influence is mediated by their making the class content interesting to students.

Beyond stimulating students in the classroom through the interesting presentation of course materials, however, faculty who were influential also seem to have made major contributions through their relationships with students outside of class. They had more out-of-class contact with students in a variety of capacities than did faculty who were not nominated as having made contributions to the students in the change group. That is, they scored higher on a measure of out-of-class contact which consisted of items concerning the number of times they had met with students in several capacities, such as discussing intellectual issues, discussing campus issues, and giving educational and career advice. Fifty-four percent of the influential teachers were high on this scale and 13 percent low; in the comparison group, 33 percent were high and 36 percent low. Of course, there is no way to tell whether the faculty members had more contact with the same students who nominated them or not, but they did report more contact with students in general.

Two important qualifications must be added. The influential faculty did not merely socialize with students any more than did their colleagues; the two groups did not differ on such items as the number of times faculty members had gone out for coffee or beer with students and attended student parties. The suspicion lingers among faculty that their colleagues who are popular with students, especially if they have much interaction with them outside the confines of the classroom, are trying to develop "buddy-buddy" relationships rather than professional teacher–student relationships. The evidence here is that the intellectually influential faculty did not cultivate these kinds of relationships any more or any less than the faculty in general. Rather, the kinds of out-of-class interactions that distinguished them from their colleagues consisted of discussions of specific issues and concerns effective teachers have always had with students.

Too, it is important to note that the intellectually influential faculty did not hold more favorable attitudes toward personalized faculty–student relationships; they did not differ from the rest of the sample on a scale called *Personalization of Faculty–Student Relations* which was composed of items such as "informal out-of-class contacts with faculty members are an important part of a student's development" and "the emotional and personal development of a student should be as important to a teacher as his intellectual development." A large majority of faculty in each group professed to believe in the value of such informal relationships among students and faculty. But, as already shown in Chapter 10, it is largely what faculty do rather than what they believe that separates the effective faculty from the others.

It would be revealing to know precisely what transpired in the out-of-class discussions among faculty and students. A key to this question may be found in the fact that the influential faculty said they talked with students more frequently about youth culture issues— drugs, sex and morality, student protest, the draft, and emerging life styles. Fifty-two percent of the influential faculty scored high on a scale concerned with the discussion of youth culture issues, compared with 34 percent of the rest of the faculty; only 20 percent were low, compared with 34 percent of the others.

This finding might lead one to conjecture that the influential faculty were more politically liberal, or radical, to have discussed such issues. But this inference is not supported by the evidence. The two groups were not different in political persuasion. Apparently the key fact is that the intellectually influential faculty were concerned about the same kinds of cultural and campus developments as the students who changed, and they were willing to discuss these developments with the students they saw outside the classroom.

In light of some recent concerns, two additional ways in which the two groups of faculty do not differ merit consideration. Although teaching and research are often said to be in essential conflict, the intellectually influential faculty had published as many articles, delivered as many papers, and authored as many books as the others.

Also, despite the idea of a generation gap between faculty and students, which found much currency in the popular literature during the 1960s, the influential faculty were distributed among age groups and academic ranks in the same proportions as their colleagues. These findings are consistent with the findings discussed in Chapter 14: scholarly productivity, age, and academic rank are not related to the amount of interaction that faculty in general have with students beyond the classroom.

It is significant, however, that the intellectually influential faculty members had different teaching assignments than their colleagues. Although only about a fourth of the total sample taught at the graduate level at all, even fewer of the intellectually influential faculty did so. But it is at the undergraduate level where the differences are most apparent. Eighty-three percent of the intellectually influential faculty taught upper division courses, as opposed to 55 percent for the comparison group. A majority of both groups also taught lower division courses, but only 18 percent of the influential faculty, compared with 36 percent of the others, did most of their teaching at that level. And a full 80 percent of the influential faculty taught independent study courses while 58 percent of their colleagues did.

It is understandable that faculty who touch the lives of undergraduate students would teach fewer graduate courses—they cannot be all things to all students. But the fact that they taught fewer lower division courses, typically introductory surveys of academic disciplines, suggests either that such courses are not appropriate vehicles for stimulating students to develop intellectually and personally or that too often they are assigned to the less competent teachers. Despite the fact that such survey courses are designed to provide a liberal education, sometimes to a captive audience, the evidence suggests that teachers of such courses are less likely to generate large amounts of intellectual stimulation. Facilitating the intellectual and personal development of students requires far more than subjecting them to a smattering of courses in the liberal arts disciplines.

On the other hand, faculty members whose teaching load is concentrated in upper division and independent study courses were more likely to be influential, perhaps in part because students are better able to pursue their own interests and to have more interaction with teachers in those learning situations. As suggested earlier, this finding may also reflect the policies of many departments to assign their best teachers to specialized upper division courses available to their major students. Not unrelated to the assignment of teachers is the common practice of providing relatively more resources for upper division than lower division instruction and permitting lower faculty–student ratios at advanced levels. Such allocation of resources virtually guarantees that lower division instruction will be less effective than upper division instruction, even though a good case could be made for the proposition that greater attention should be given to less experienced students. Whatever the reasons may be, the fact remains that intellectual influence is more often mediated through upper division and independent study courses than through lower division ones.

Whatever they may give to students, the influential faculty appear to receive certain benefits from their efforts. They enjoy reputations as effective teachers among their colleagues; they were more likely than the comparison groups to have been named by one or more of their colleagues as both outstanding teachers and as persons who have significant impact on the lives of students. They also perceived that they have more influence on students: they scored higher on a scale of *Self-Perceived Influence* which concerns students in general; they were more likely to name students to whose educational or personal development they had contributed a great deal; and they thought they had more influence on those particular students than did the comparison group of faculty. Their favorable reputation among their students and colleagues and their self-recognized influence on students must give the influential faculty a great sense of personal satisfaction. Indeed, it may be that such results are so gratifying to faculty members that they become even more committed to undergraduate teaching, the first characteristic mentioned that distinguishes the intellectually influential faculty.

STUDENTS WHO CHANGE AND INFLUENTIAL FACULTY

From these two analyses, it is apparent that the students who actually become more intellectually oriented and the teachers who helped them are quite similar. Students who changed recognized that they had grown in a number of cognitive and affective ways, while influential faculty realized that they had had much impact on the lives of students. Although students who changed were interested in ideas, especially ideas with a personal reference, they had not derived any more from course work outside their major field than students who did not change. And although influential faculty were interested in teaching, they were distinguished in their classroom teaching primarily by their attempts to make the content interesting to students.

Students who changed were more heavily influenced by independent study and courses in their majors, and influential faculty more frequently taught independent study and upper division courses. The students who changed were heavily involved in youth culture activities—artistic, intellectual, activist, and hip nonconformist—while the intellectually stimulating faculty they named discussed those youth culture issues with students frequently. The students who changed had much interaction with faculty outside of class, while the influential faculty had much out-of-class contact with students. Thus, students who became more intellectually oriented and the influential faculty who stimulated them intellectually seem to have found each other, formed productive faculty–student relationships, and realized the ideal of effective teaching and learning inherent in the concept of a liberal education.

Chapter 14

Faculty–Student Interaction Beyond the Classroom

The importance of out-of-class interaction was demonstrated in the preceding chapter. Faculty who were nominated by their students and colleagues as especially effective reported more interaction with students beyond the classroom; students who increased in intellectual disposition reported more contact with faculty as a part of their more aggressive use of the educational resources of the college generally; and, out-of-class interaction has been shown to be related to particular kinds of influence. These findings suggest that the relationships that faculty and students develop outside the classroom may well be the part of teaching which has the greatest impact on students.

Close and frequent interaction between students and teachers has long been held to be a central value of education, whether as a means by which the transmission of knowledge is best facilitated or as an educational goal in and of itself. Research, however, has shown out-of-class interaction to be fairly infrequent and superficial in most institutions of higher learning (Feldman & Newcomb, 1969). Much less has been done to investigate factors that tend to facilitate or impede such interaction, and little is known about the consequences of faculty–student interaction, even though much has been written and said in its support.

Some of the characteristics of institutions, faculty, and students that might facilitate or impede out-of-class interaction between students and faculty are analyzed in this chapter. The possible beneficial consequences of interaction, both to students and to faculty, are also explored. It is hoped that these data will contribute substantially to a practical understanding of the nature and consequences of faculty–student interaction beyond the classroom.

THE NATURE AND INCIDENCE OF INTERACTION

The measure of interaction used in this study is based on a summation score of the frequency with which individual faculty members and students reported having engaged in six kinds of out-of-class discussions; that is, the total number of discussions students reported with faculty and faculty reported with students. The six discussion areas were selected because they were all considered to be potential aspects of typical faculty–student relationships, and because they were found to be important variables in Study I. The six discussion areas are: intellectual issues or course-related matters; educational plans or advice; informal conversations or socializing; career plans or advice; campus issues or sociopolitical discourse; and personal problems or counseling. The frequencies for each type of interaction—as reported by faculty and by students—appear in Table 1.

While it was the rare teacher indeed who reported having met with *no* undergraduates to discuss intellectual or course-related matters (certainly a primary conversational concern of faculty–student relationships), less than one-half (47 percent) of the faculty saw five or more students for that purpose during the two-week period. And as Table 1 shows only between 15 and 53 percent of the faculty saw as many as *three* students in each of the other five discussion areas during that time. Even a conservative estimate of the number of students a teacher faces in his classes (as well as in his capacity as advisor, independent-studies sponsor, and in other nonclassroom teaching roles) would suggest that the potential for interaction with students beyond the classroom is considerably greater than its actual incidence. Even if a teacher did not encourage students to come to see him at least once during a school term (and 73 percent of the faculty reported that they did follow such a practice), one would expect him to be sought out by more students than these figures indicate.* Clearly there must be some barriers to faculty–student interaction beyond the classroom.

---

* It should be pointed out that the two-week period reported on was in almost all cases a period within the school term, rather than at the very beginning or end of it. Initial mailings of the faculty questionnaire were made four to five weeks into the school term at each institution, and the bulk of completed returns received within two to three weeks thereafter.

Table 1 Frequency of Faculty–Student Interaction in Six Discussion Areas, as Reported by Faculty and Students, in percentages

Discussions about:	Number of Different Discussions of 10 Minutes or More with Undergraduates during a Two-Week Period				Number or Different Discussions of 10 Minutes or More with Faculty Members during a One-Month Period			
	None	1–2	3 or more	Total[a]	None	1–2	3 or more	Total[a]
Intellectual issues or course-related matters	3	19	78	100	36	39	24	99
Educational plans or advice	15	32	53	100	29	46	25	100
Informal conversations or socializing	20	32	48	100	34	35	30	99
Career plans or advice	19	43	38	100	33	44	23	100
Campus issues or sociopolitical discourse	37	34	29	100	53	31	16	100
Personal problems or counseling	43	42	15	100	78	18	4	100

[a] Total percentages vary because all percentages rounded to nearest whole number.

153

When attention is turned to student reports of out-of-class contacts with faculty, it becomes even more apparent that such contacts were very infrequent. Indeed, the percentage of students reporting *no* out-of-class discussions in each of the six areas ranges from 29 to 78 percent. Yet the period covered by the student questionnaire was a *month*, rather than the lesser two-week period reported on by faculty members.

It would appear that even in their senior year, then, most students have had only a modest amount of contact with their teachers outside the classroom. More importantly, the range of interaction is such that some students have had very little or no contact, while others have reported repeated and varied discussions with faculty. Likewise, there are some faculty members who reported many contacts with students over the six discussion areas, and there are those faculty who indicated that their contacts with students outside the classroom for any discussion purpose were few and far between. By comparing the attitudes, behaviors, and experiences of those faculty and students who have interacted most frequently with those who have interacted least frequently, it was hoped that the characteristics of each that seemed to facilitate interaction might be revealed. Thus, in order to explore and to test hypotheses about the major impediments to and facilitators and consequents of faculty–student interaction, faculty and students were each divided into three approximately equal-sized groups on the bases of their summated frequencies of reported out-of-class interaction over the six discussion areas. The groups are: high-interactors, medium-interactors, and low-interactors.*

FACTORS THAT FACILITATE OR IMPEDE FACULTY–STUDENT INTERACTION OUTSIDE THE CLASSROOM

Before exploring the differential personal characteristics of high- and low-interactors among faculty and students it is important to confront the institutional factors, especially size and internal structure, often held to be responsible for impeding or facilitating faculty–student interaction. Once the effects of institutions on the frequency of faculty–student interaction are better understood, it is possible to focus on the personal characteristics of high- and low-interactors that

* There were 229 high-interacting faculty (scores of 11 to 18); 227 medium-interacting faculty (scores of 7 to 10); and 183 low-interacting faculty (scores of 0 to 6). Students were divided into 439 high-interactors (scores of 7 to 18); 588 medium-interactors (scores of 3 to 6); and 413 low-interactors (scores of 0 to 2).

seem to affect their interaction patterns regardless of the institutional setting.

Institutional Factors The frequency with which students interact with faculty outside the classroom is affected by many factors. One of the most important of these is unquestionably the kind of college or university attended. Differences between institutional settings— including size, faculty–student ratio, educational philosophy, internal organization, and overall student and faculty norms of interaction— may be expected to operate as significant aids or barriers to faculty–student contact beyond the classroom (see Chapter 15).

At the largest institution in the sample, the University of California at Berkeley (from which about one-half of the students and more than one-third of the faculty in the sample were drawn), both faculty and students reported significantly less interaction with one another beyond the classroom than is true at any of the other seven institutions singly or combined. At the other seven schools, taken as a group, about twice the proportion of students interacted frequently with faculty. The student experience, in fact, is almost exactly reversed between Berkeley and the other institutions. Among the Berkeley students, only 20 percent reported frequent interaction, and 39 percent reported very infrequent interaction with faculty; at the other institutions, combined, 40 percent of the students reported frequent interaction, and only 20 percent had little or no contact with faculty. Comparable though smaller differences were also found in the frequency of interaction reported by faculty at the two types of institutions.

Evidence that large institutions can at least partially overcome the barriers of size through the creation of differentiated internal structures designed to bring faculty and students together, such as cluster colleges, was also found. The percentage of students who experienced frequent interaction with faculty (with one exception) is about the same at the cluster colleges within moderate-sized universities as it is at the small liberal arts colleges long heralded for their close faculty–student interaction. Small, autonomous liberal arts colleges, however, may have an edge over cluster colleges in reducing the percentage of students who have little or no contact with faculty. While the cluster-college arrangement seems to increase the possibility for faculty–student interaction for some students, it by no means guarantees it for all.

There is considerable diversity among the seven smaller institutions included in this study in terms of such factors as size, academic reputation, educational philosophy and purpose, and the like. However, minor differences in the amount and kinds of interaction experienced by their faculties and students pale when they are contrasted with the experience of faculty and students at Berkeley, a much larger, research-oriented university.

Characteristics of Students   We began this study with certain ideas as to the kind of students who might be expected to interact most frequently with faculty outside the classroom. One set of factors expected to be important had to do with students' living arrangements and the number of years or hours per week they were employed while attending college. It was reasoned that students who lived off-campus or who had to work any appreciable amount of time while attending school would have less opportunity for getting to know faculty members outside the classroom. This did not seem to be the case. Neither living arrangements nor the number of hours worked per week differed significantly for students of different interaction levels. Interestingly, high-interactors were in fact more often employed during some portion of their college careers and, when employed, had worked for a greater proportion of their school years. One possible explanation for this apparent anomaly is that high-interacting students more often reported having worked for faculty members, grading papers, tutoring, or doing research than did other students. Fifty-four percent of them had done so at least once, compared to only 17 percent of the low-interactors, and fully 36 percent had done so twice or more, compared to only seven percent of the low-interactors. This means that at least for a significant proportion of the high-interactors their employment not only did not impede their interaction with faculty but facilitated it—indeed, in some cases perhaps, constituted it.

A second set of factors expected to be associated with interaction with faculty consisted of student interests, attitudes, and behavior patterns that might be considered on an a priori basis to be similar to or highly compatible with the interests, attitudes, and behavior patterns of most faculty. High-interacting students did in fact evidence a tendency as freshmen to be somewhat more like faculty. For example, they more often reported reading books for pleasure, expected artistic and cultural interests to be of greater importance to them, more often reported liking to write papers, and indeed more often expressed a desire to become a college teacher than did their low-interacting peers. As will be pointed out, the similarities between high-interacting students and faculty become even more pronounced by the time the students are seniors.

High-interacting students differ from their peers in that they more aggressively pursue their own educational interests during their college years. They more often initiate courses, take exams in lieu of required courses, participate in group study, and take independent study courses. They also speak out considerably more often in class, or at least in their favorite classes. This suggests that one of the major barriers to interaction with faculty is a student's own inability or unwillingness to initiate out-of-class contacts with his teachers; the low-interactor plays a less active role in his own education.

Characteristics of Faculty   In the first study (Chapter 4) we found that faculty members who interacted the most frequently with their students outside the classroom held more favorable views of students generally, and they more often endorsed statements reflecting an educational philosophy that stresses faculty–student interaction and faculty concern for the whole student. The interpretation made in Study I was that these faculty attitudes are communicated to students through a variety of cues, including the ways in which a teacher goes about his teaching inside the classroom, and that students use such cues in assessing the degree to which a teacher is interested in what students think as well as his openness to interaction with them. Attitudes and behaviors found to be associated with out-of-class contact with students were termed aspects of a teacher's social-psychological accessibility to students, and evidence was marshalled for the hypothesis that students more often seek out those faculty who appear by their attitudes and in-class teaching practices to be the most open and accessible for interaction with students beyond the classroom.

The hypothesis that the more accessible the teacher the more interaction he will have with students outside the classroom is supported by the faculty data in this study as well. High-interacting faculty more often endorsed such statements as "students learn best if a teacher takes a personal interest in them," and "informal out-of-class contacts with faculty members are an important part of a student's development." Items such as these form a *Personalization of Faculty–Student Relations* scale. Faculty who interacted most with students also reportedly talked more with students, both in and out of class, about issues of contemporary interest and even urgency to students, such as drugs, sex, emerging life styles, the draft, and student protests that took place on their own campuses.

Faculty who most frequently interact with students outside the classroom not only appear to students to be more accessible *psychologically,* they also make themselves more *physically* available to them beyond their classrooms or faculty offices: they more often reported that they attended student parties and meetings and that they could be found in such places as the student lounge or cafeteria.

Within the classroom, high-interactors also differed in the actual conduct of their classes. By their own report, they strive to be more dynamic, interesting, even showmanlike in their course presentations. For example, they more often said that they tell humorous stories, anecdotes, and jokes, and use stories and analogies to illuminate points they make in class. Items such as these are part of the *Presentation Interest* scale. High-interactors also more often encouraged and provided for student participation in their courses by inviting student criticism of ideas and student evaluations of the course, and by giving students the responsibility for presenting topics, conducting panels, or leading class discussions, and the opportunity to share their knowledge or experience with the classes. Items such as these form the *Student Participation* scale.

High-interacting faculty are also more discursive in their approach to subject matter, which no doubt suggests to students a wider range of subjects that might be profitably pursued with such faculty members. High-interacting faculty more often reported that they relate the course work to other fields of study and to current social problems and that they more often discuss points of view other than their own in their classes. Responses to items such as these form the teaching practices scale called *Discursiveness*.

No less important for understanding faculty–student interaction are those characteristics of faculty found not to be related to the amount of interaction that a faculty member had with students beyond the normal classroom situation. Among them are age, rank, years of teaching experience, research productivity, political affiliations and self-designations (the radical-liberal-conservative spectrum), the degree of permissiveness of or support for student social freedoms (in matters of dress, living arrangements, use of alcohol or drugs) or tolerance or support for faculty or student activism. Academic discipline was related only in that natural scientists reported somewhat less interaction with students and less often shared the attitudes or evidenced the behaviors associated with it.

THE CONSEQUENCES OF INTERACTION FOR STUDENTS

One of the least surprising consequences of frequent personal interaction with faculty is that students develop further their interest in and commitment to intellectual concerns. As noted earlier, students who interact the most frequently with faculty differ somewhat from their peers even as freshmen. From the very beginning they share many intellectual interests, attitudes, and proclivities with faculty, and one of the major effects of their college experience—and inferentially of their greater interaction with faculty—is to accentuate those interests and concerns. For example, high-interacting students as seniors, when compared with their peers, read more books for pleasure, spent more hours per week studying, reported considerably more satisfaction from independent studies, more often expected to go on for a PhD, and characterized their ideal college as having a highly rigorous academic program rather than one of only moderate difficulty.

High-interacting students also perceive that they have made more progress in a variety of specific academic skills than have other students (see Table 2). For example, they feel that they have increased their knowledge both of specifics, such as terminology or trends, and of universals and abstractions in a field. They feel that they have increased their ability to comprehend or interpret, to evaluate material and methods, and to apply abstractions or principles to a particular situation. These academic skills are, of course, the stock-in-trade of faculty and among the chief wares they offer to students. Students who have the most contact with faculty no doubt put a greater premium on such skills due to their greater initial intellectual orientation, but it is not unreasonable to assume that they also in fact benefit more from that interaction in making progress in these skill areas. Twenty-nine percent of the high-interacting students did in fact report five or more discussions with faculty members about academic or intellectual issues, and only 4 percent of them had no discussions of this kind during the one-month period. On the other hand, none of the low-interactors had five or more academic discussions, and fully 81 percent reported none at all during the one-month period in question. So it is important to note that low-interacting students not only report infrequent out-of-class contact with faculty over a wide range of discussion topics, but more specifically they report little or no personal exchange with faculty on topics central to the acquisition of academic skills.

Low-interacting students also had much less contact with the one faculty member who was named as most important to them. Forty-four percent of the low-interacting students said that they had seldom or never had any contact with their most impactful faculty member outside the classroom; 45 percent had had only occasional

Table 2 The Outcome of Interaction for Students: Characteristics of Students as Seniors by Three Levels of Interaction with Faculty, in percentages

	Students		
	Low-Interactors	Medium-Interactors	High-Interactors
As seniors report having made "much progress" in:			
Knowledge or specifics of a field	56	57	68
Knowledge of universals and abstractions in a field	43	48	58
Ability to comprehend, interpret, or extrapolate	49	57	65
Ability to evaluate materials and methods	48	57	67
Ability to apply abstraction or principles	41	46	59
Frequency of out-of-class contacts with most impactful teacher:			
Seldom or never	44	23	12
Occasionally	45	50	37
Quite often or frequently	11	27	51
Named a faculty member as "the one faculty member who contributed most to your educational and/or personal development"	66	80	84
Named a faculty member as having "played a role in your choice of major"	14	24	30
Expected and actual importance of satisfaction received from getting to know faculty members:			
As freshmen (expected)	41	43	49
As seniors (actual)	9	24	45

contact; and only 11 percent had quite often or frequently had such contact. Among high-interacting students the experience is reversed: 51 percent of the high-interactors said that they had quite often or frequently had out-of-class discussions with the faculty members of greatest importance to them, and only 12 percent had never or seldom experienced such contact (see Table 2).

In light of their meager interaction experiences, it is not surprising that low-interacting students less often even named a faculty member who had contributed most to their educational or personal development. Whereas only 66 percent of the low-interactors named such a faculty member, 84 percent of the high-interacting students did so. It seems likely that this difference is primarily (although not wholly) attributable to the fact that because these students had so little contact with any faculty member it was difficult for them to feel that any teacher had made an important contribution to them. In this regard, it is important to note that low-interacting students were not more reluctant to name the teacher of the most stimulating course they had taken during their four years in college. Ninety-seven percent of the low-interacting students named such a course and teacher, and 99 percent of the high-interacting students did so.

High-interacting students also more often named a faculty member as having influenced their choice of major and said that one of the reasons for their choice of major was that faculty had encouraged them. These are rather specific aspects of faculty influence, and it is instructive to note that their incidence is increased by the total amount of interaction a student had with faculty generally. In other words, it seems that the more interaction with faculty a student has generally, the greater is the probability that one or more of those teachers will have some kind of specific impact on him. While such a finding is of the mundane, common-sense variety, it is nevertheless convincing evidence of the potency of close faculty–student interaction for having these kinds of impact on a student.

There are still other consequences of interaction to students. High-interacting seniors expressed a greater satisfaction with the total college experience and with virtually all specific aspects of it. Of these the most dramatic difference appears in regard to interaction itself. For example, 45 percent of the high-interactors, but only 9 percent of the low-interactors felt as seniors that getting to know faculty members had been important for them. Comparisons between freshmen expectations and senior retrospections reveal that the gap is quite wide for low-interactors, whereas high-interactors seem to have come much closer to realizing their expectations, especially in those areas heavily dependent on interpersonal relationships (see Table 2).

High-interacting students seem to feel that they are more "together" than do low-interactors. They seem to have a greater sense of who they are and where they are going, both personally and vocationally. They feel that they have increased more in self-awareness, in the firmness of their sense of identity, in their ability to form close relationships, and in their commitment both to life styles and to vocations. As seniors 89 percent of the high-interactors had chosen occupations, whereas 76 percent of the low-interactors had done so; and 48 percent of the high-interactors felt that their choice was very definite, whereas only 35 percent of the low-interactors were that certain of the vocations they had chosen. It is interesting to note that these choices were differentially made during college rather than prior to it; as freshmen, the proportion of students in each of the groups who had made vocational decisions did not differ significantly.

High-interacting students also report that they are more often sought out by other students for knowledge, advice, or opinion regarding their course work or instructors. Sixty-seven percent of the high-interactors—and only 32 percent of the low-interactors—reported that this occurred often or very often. While this student-to-student interaction may reflect these students' greater sociability generally, it is also likely that it is to some degree a reflection of a general student awareness that high-interactors are more involved with faculty and somewhat more like them in academic orientation and skills, therefore making good stand-ins for them. It may be that, to an appreciable extent, these high-interacting students serve as intermediaries between faculty and other students; for many students the knowledge and skills that faculty offer may come to them not so much directly as indirectly, through a kind of two-step flow of information. Katz and Lazarsfeld (1955) have shown that there are individuals in any community who, being themselves more in touch with what is going on in various aspects of American culture, are sought out by others for advice, information, and opinions. For many individuals, knowledge that can be gained by close attention to the various media or through close association with taste makers and decision makers is sought instead, from individuals in the community known to have wide exposure to the media and/or to various kinds of elites in the community. Students who have frequent contact with faculty may acquire personal influence among their peers in much the same fashion and for much the same reason.

THE CONSEQUENCES OF INTERACTION FOR FACULTY

Perhaps the greatest concomitant of interaction for faculty is their greater sense of effectiveness in dealing with students. High-interacting faculty perceive that they have greater influence on students generally in three major areas: students' personal philosophies, decisions about majors, and formulation of career plans. Forty percent of the high-interactors felt that they had quite a bit or a great deal of influence in helping students to develop their personal philosophies or outlooks on life, whereas only 19 percent of the low-interactors felt that they had that kind of impact on the students with whom they had had personal contact. Similarly, 59 percent of the high-interactors felt that they had had quite a bit or a great deal of influence in helping students to make decisions about their major fields of study, compared to only 35 percent of the low-interactors. In the area of influencing students by helping them to formulate their career plans, 49 percent of the high-interactors and only 22 percent of the low-interactors felt that they had had some appreciable impact.

This sense of potency is not restricted to their generalized relationship with students (where the sheer numbers of students influenced may contribute to the sense of influence); high-interacting faculty also felt that they had had considerably greater influence on the one student to whose educational or personal development they felt they had contributed a great deal, especially in the area of helping him to develop a personal philosophy or outlook on life. Indeed, they significantly more often named students in this category than did the low-interactors. This would suggest that the greater potency, effectiveness, or influence which high-interacting faculty feel that they have on students is a qualitative as well as a quantitative phenomenon. It is not only because they have more contact with a greater number of students that they feel they have more impact in certain areas of student development; they also feel that they have had more impact on individual students whom they have named as having benefited most from their help or attention.

Most important of all, the potency or impactfulness of high-interacting faculty is not only a self-perceived quality—it is perceived by others as well. As can be seen in Table 3, faculty who by their own self-report had the most frequent out-of-class interaction with students significantly more often received nominations by students as "the *one* faculty member at this institution who you feel has contributed *most* to your educational and/or personal development." They also significantly more often received nomina-

Table 3   The Outcome of Interaction for Faculty: Faculty Characteristics by Three Levels of Interaction with Students, in percentages

	Faculty		
	Low-Interactors	Medium-Interactors	High-Interactors
Received one or more nominations by students as the *one* faculty member who contributed *most* to their development	20	29	35
Received one or more nominations by students as having influenced their choice of major	5	9	21
Received one or more nominations by colleagues as an "outstanding teacher"	27	30	48
Received one or more nominations by colleagues as a teacher who has "significant impact on the lives of students"	11	18	41

tions by students as a faculty member who "played a role in your choice of major." Nor is their greater impact or effectiveness perceived only by students. High-interacting faculty also receive more nominations by their colleagues as outstanding teachers at their institutions, and as the one faculty member at their institution who seem to have "significant impact on the lives of students."

Thus it seems clear that out-of-class interaction does have appreciable positive consequences to faculty as well as to students. Faculty who reported that they have had frequent contact with students outside the classroom not only have a greater sense of their own personal effectiveness, but they are perceived by students to have had greater impact on their educational and personal development and are perceived by their colleagues to be both superior teachers and to have the most significant impact on the lives of students. They appear both to communicate their greater accessibility for interaction to their students and to make themselves more visibly effective to their colleagues.

High-interacting faculty differed in another way, too, a way that has considerable implication for the improvement of college teaching:

they indicated greater support for formal procedures for evaluating teaching effectiveness. Seventy-nine percent of the high-interacting faculty, compared to only 59 percent of the low-interactors, felt that there should be such evaluation procedures, and among the high-interactors there was also more support for the idea that students should play a primary role in such evaluations. Since teaching evaluation might be expected to include measures of teachers' interaction with students, those faculty who do interact and who do evidence their accessibility to students both inside and outside the classroom might well expect that they would come out fairly well on evaluation of teaching. On the other hand, faculty who do not interact frequently and who demonstrate their relative inaccessibility in a variety of ways may well fear such evaluation, especially if students played a primary role in it. One of the major consequences of interaction to faculty would seem to be strong, confident self-images as effective teachers, making the high-interacting faculty members less fearful of evaluation by a relevant constituency.

It should be recalled that our first study reported other concomitants of interaction for faculty which included a greater sense of satisfaction with stimulation received from students, a belief that students regard them among the very best of teachers on their campuses, and greater knowledge about the academic strengths and weaknesses of students at their schools.

CONCLUSION

High-interacting students, in general, seem to take a far more active role in their own education than do their peers. Not only are they more interested in pursuing their own intellectual interests, but they are more actively engaged in utilizing the existing resources and structures of their institutions and in changing them in directions that respond better to their needs. As the data have shown, these students more often helped initiate new courses, took exams in lieu of required courses, participated in study groups among some of the students in classes, took independent study courses, served on faculty–student committees within colleges or departments, and used the available counseling services. They also spoke out the most frequently in the courses which they most enjoyed.

In an important sense, seeking out faculty members for discussion outside the classroom is also illustrative of these students' tendency to take a more active role in determining their own education. Indeed, others (Dienst, 1971) have found that students' activist orientation toward politics is also positively related to the amount of interaction with faculty. One might conclude from these findings that there are students who take considerable initiative and responsibility for their own learning experiences and that there are those who do not, that there is little hope of making the second type over into the first. If the characteristics of students were the only factors involved in faculty–student interaction, that might be a reasonable conclusion. As has been shown, however, the institution itself—because of its size, internal structure, and interaction values and norms—affects the interaction patterns of both faculty and students. Likewise, interaction, because it is a two-way process, does not depend solely on the attitudes or behavior patterns of students; it is also heavily influenced by the interaction values and behaviors of faculty which encourage or discourage students of whatever character to seek them out beyond the classroom setting. It is quite probable that faculty–student interaction can be increased significantly by careful attention to the interplay of these three major components—faculty, students, and setting. The influence of setting, or context, on interaction is examined in the next chapter.

Chapter 15

Contextual Milieus for Teaching and Learning

A number of characteristics of faculty and students have repeatedly emerged as factors in effective teaching and learning. Faculty who make a significant impact on at least some of their students have been found to be more committed to teaching and appear to give more of themselves in terms of time, energy, and abilities in order to be effective with students. Students who evidence the most progress in their intellectual or personal growth also appear to have been the most committed to certain kinds of learning and areas of personal development and to have taken more active roles in seeking out effective learning experiences during their college years. Repeatedly, one of the overriding differences found between faculty and students who engage in effective teaching and learning and those who do not was *the amount of interaction*—both inside and outside the classroom—that students and teachers have with one another.

So far, only minimal attention has been given to institutional differences in the incidence of the teaching and learning behaviors shown to be effective. Interest has been focused on discovering the characteristics and correlates of growth-producing teaching and learning, regardless of the setting in which they occur. Yet it is widely recognized that the specific policies, procedures, and organizational structures of a college or university can operate to either facilitate or impede certain kinds of teaching and learning, including many of those that this study has found to be highly effective.

High on the list of characteristics of institutions that affect teaching and learning is what sociologists refer to as the normative climate created by faculty and students themselves. This contexual milieu is of greatest concern here: institutional variation in the incidence of certain key characteristics of effective teaching and learning will be set forth and analyzed along with some related attitudes, values, and behaviors that help to explain those institutional differences. Since faculty–student interaction has been found to be such a pervasive characteristic of effective teaching and learning, the discussion will begin by summarizing institutional differences in out-of-class interaction and will proceed to analyze the values and expectations for interaction held by students and faculty at different kinds of institutions. Institutional differences in other teaching and learning experiences will also be explored, largely as they relate to the central factor of interaction.

Because the greatest institutional differences in the out-of-class interaction experiences of both faculty and students were found between the University of California at Berkeley and the other institutions in the study, much of the presentation will be made in terms of the Berkeley data versus the data from all the other institutions combined.* In combining the other institutions and presenting their faculty and student data collectively, it is possible to materially reduce and simplify the presentation of institutional differences without losing much either in information or accuracy. Important and statistically significant differences found between the experiences of faculty and students at the other institutions will be mentioned.

INSTITUTIONAL DIFFERENCES IN THE INTERACTIONAL EXPERIENCES OF STUDENTS

There was a near reversal of faculty and student interaction experiences at Berkeley in comparison to the other institutions combined. Figure 1 shows that only 20 percent of the Berkeley students experienced relatively frequent out-of-class interaction with faculty (more than seven contacts during a month), while at the other

---

* For certain of the student data, the two colleges within the University of the Pacific—Raymond College and College of the Pacific—are treated separately, thus providing nine institutional settings instead of eight. Because Raymond College has a three-year undergraduate program, Raymond students as seniors were actually studied in the third year of the research project; consequently, for some questions, which were added to the senior questionnaire in the fourth year of the study, Raymond data is not available. For the faculty data, University of the Pacific is considered a single institution, with Raymond College and College of the Pacific faculties combined.

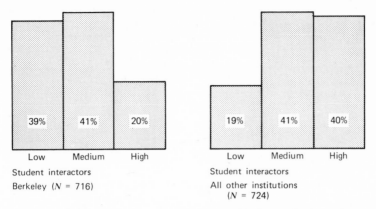

Figure 1.   Percentage of students at Berkeley and at all other institutions who reported low, medium, and high amounts of interaction with faculty outside the classroom.

institutions 40 percent of the students had done so. Similarly, 39 percent of the Berkeley students had little or no interaction with faculty beyond the classroom (two or fewer contacts during a month), compared to only 19 percent of the students at the other institutions.

It might be reasonable to attribute the infrequent interaction of Berkeley students with their teachers to the much greater size of the Berkeley campus, but size alone—in sheer press of student num- bers—should, if anything, increase the amount of interaction which Berkeley faculty experience with their students. That is to say, while it is easy to see how a large student body may decrease the individual student's opportunities for conferring with overburdened faculty members, the individual teacher on a large campus should experience a great deal of interaction with students even if he never sees the same student twice. Yet, as can be seen in Figure 2, Berkeley faculty also experience much less interaction outside the classroom. Like their students, only 20 percent of the Berkeley faculty see students relatively frequently outside the classroom (11 or more contacts during a two-week period), and 36 percent see them quite infrequently, if at all (six or fewer contacts during a two-week pe- riod). At the other institutions, faculty are more evenly divided between high-, medium-, and low-interactors.

It seems unlikely, then, that size alone can explain the uniqueness of the Berkeley experience. One must turn to the normative climates of students and faculty to find satisfactory explanations for such insti- tutional differences. Perhaps Berkeley students and faculty value such interaction less. If faculty–student interaction is neither desired nor

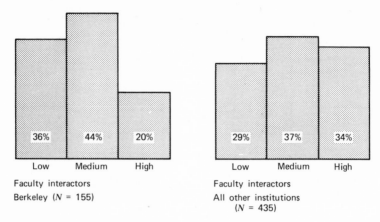

Figure 2.   Percentage of faculty at Berkeley and at all other institutions who reported low, medium, and high amounts of interaction with students outside the classroom.

felt to be desirable at Berkeley, while being held in some esteem elsewhere, the differential experiences could be accounted for in terms of the different contextual milieu of the institutions.

It seems a reasonable hypothesis, in fact, that students who enter large, prestigious public universities like Berkeley do not expect, or perhaps do not desire, close interaction with faculty. It might even be the case that these students so differ in interpersonal needs and styles from students who elect to attend smaller, less impersonal institutions that the paucity of out-of-class interaction experienced by them neither distresses them emotionally nor deters their intellectual growth.

While such a hypothesis may appear to have merit, it is not wholly supported by the data. Freshmen at Berkeley significantly less often characterized their ideal college as a close-knit community than did students elsewhere, but a full 75 percent of them still felt that community was an ideal quality. Because they chose to attend a school widely known for its lack of community, the question arises, then, whether they misperceived the true nature of the institution in which they were enrolled. The data suggest that the answer is both yes and no. The fact that less than 10 percent of the Berkeley students said that a closely-knit community, with a chance to know students and faculty, was an important consideration in selecting that institution (compared to 63 percent of the students at the other institutions who cited this as a reason for their choice of school) would suggest that they were far from unaware of the more impersonal nature of the university they elected to attend. Likewise, both as freshman and as seniors, Berkeley students were the least likely of any students to say that an ideal college would be characterized by a small student body. Only about a quarter of the Berkeley students, as freshmen and again as seniors, felt that a small student body was ideal, whereas between 50 and 98 percent of the students at the other institutions, either as freshmen or as seniors, felt that to be a desirable characteristic of a college or university.

But at the same time, many of the Berkeley freshmen seemed to have held quite unrealistic personal expectations regarding the possibilities for their own interaction with faculty. For example, 45 percent of the Berkeley freshmen expected that getting to know faculty would be more than somewhat important in terms of their own personal satisfaction during their undergraduate years. This percentage does not differ significantly from the 43 percent of students attending smaller and less impersonal institutions who also expected interaction with faculty to be important.

In the expectations of freshmen attending the other institutions, however, there was also considerable institutional variation. Sixty-three percent of the Santa Cruz students and 68 percent of the Raymond students, for example, expected that getting to know faculty would be important, compared to only 45 percent of the students at both Berkeley and the College of the Pacific. The fact that the Santa Cruz campus is composed of several cluster colleges, while Berkeley is not, and Raymond is a small cluster college within the larger University of the Pacific illustrates the greater interaction expectations of students attending different campuses or subcolleges of the same institutions. At Monteith, however, which is another cluster college (at Wayne State University), only 41 percent of the students expected such interaction to be important. This suggests that the chance to get to know faculty members is not an equally strong attraction of all cluster colleges, although it may be important at most. Since students elsewhere within Wayne State University were not included in this study, we cannot be certain that the interaction expectations of Monteith freshmen—although low—are not higher than for the campus as a whole.

It would appear then that as entering freshmen Berkeley students did not differ dramatically from students at other institutions (except some cluster colleges) in the value they placed on faculty–student interaction or in their personal expectations for getting to know faculty members. Yet as seniors, they did differ strikingly in the amount of out-of-class interaction they actually experienced. The percentage of students reporting high, medium, and low levels of interaction with faculty is shown for each institution separately in Table 1.

Furthermore, Berkeley seniors also differed significantly in the extent to which they had experienced other kinds of learning experiences. They took a less active role in initiating courses, for instance: only 14 percent of the Berkeley students had participated in initiating courses, whereas the percentage of students who did so at the other institutions ranged from a low of 22 percent at Luther to a high of 46 percent at Santa Cruz. Unfortunately, data from Raymond students is missing for this item, but at both of the other two cluster colleges—with reputations for being experimental—a higher percentage of students engaged in course initiation than at most institutions. Interestingly, Berkeley students also interacted with their peers less, at least in educationally relevant ways: only 56 percent of the Berkeley students had ever participated in study groups, whereas at all of the other institutions (except Shimer where students also

Table 1 Percentage of Students at Each Institution Who Reported Low, Medium, or High Levels of Interaction with Faculty Outside the Classroom

Institutions	Students			
	Low-Interactors	Medium-Interactors	High-Interactors	N
Clark College	8	44	49	39
Shimer College	13	47	46	24
Raymond College, University of the Pacific	22	33	45	49
Northeastern Illinois State College	21	37	42	199
College of the Pacific, University of the Pacific	20	40	40	92
Stevenson College, University of California at Santa Cruz	26	39	40	88
Luther College	16	46	38	204
Monteith College, Wayne State University	24	48	28	29
University of California at Berkeley	39	41	20	716
				1440

tended to be intellectual loners in this regard) three-quarters or more of the students had done so.

Berkeley students also less often interacted with their teachers inside the classroom than did students elsewhere. When asked to say how often they had spoken out in their favorite classes to ask questions, volunteer answers, or make comments, 48 percent of the Berkeley students reported having done so four times or more. The percentage at the other schools ranged from a low of 53 percent at College of the Pacific to a high of 96 percent at Shimer.

Even the nature of a student's relationship with the one faculty member he named as having contributed the most to his own educational or personal development differed at Berkeley. For example, 24 percent of the Berkeley students reported that they had met quite often or frequently with the faculty members whose impact had been greatest on them personally, and 30 percent had seldom or never done so. At the other institutions, however, 37 percent of the students had quite often or frequently met with their most impactful teachers, and only 19 percent had seldom or never done so.

Thus it is apparent that there is considerable institutional variation in the amount and kinds of learning experiences students have, including those that have been repeatedly shown in this study to be especially effective in promoting intellectual and personal growth. It is also apparent that the learning experiences of Berkeley students differed considerably from those of students elsewhere. To the extent that the Berkeley data may be typical of very large public, research-oriented universities, these differences have particularly important implications for improving undergraduate instruction at such institutions.

INSTITUTIONAL DIFFERENCES IN THE INTERACTIONAL EXPERIENCES OF FACULTY

Not surprisingly, there is also considerable institutional variation in the teaching experiences of faculties. They differ in the extent to which they value interaction with students, are committed to undergraduate teaching generally, and make extra efforts to be accessible and even to reach out to their students. There is more institutional variation in actual faculty behavior than in faculty ideology about the value of interaction with students, however. For example, if responses of faculty to the item, "informal out-of-class contacts with faculty are an important part of a student's development" are analyzed, only 40 percent of the Berkeley faculty and 47 percent of the faculties of the other institutions agreed strongly with the statement. On the other hand, when asked if they were available whenever students want to talk, only 30 percent of the Berkeley faculty compared with 49 percent of the faculty elsewhere indicated that they made themselves available in this way.

It is noteworthy that faculty assessments of the importance of interaction with faculty in facilitating student development exceed those of students. Fifty-six percent of the Berkeley faculty and 60 percent of the faculty at the other institutions felt that getting to know faculty had been of great or considerable importance to students' overall education and development at their institutions. Only 21 percent of the Berkeley students and 31 percent of the students elsewhere, however, felt that getting to know faculty had been important in terms of their own personal satisfactions with the college experience.

Indeed, students generally do not seem to feel that most faculty have any real interest in students and their problems. And as Figure 3 illustrates, seniors' assessment of faculty concern is related not only to the amount of out-of-class interaction they personally experienced with faculty, but also to the interaction norms of the institution they attended. Again, the differences between Berkeley and the other in-

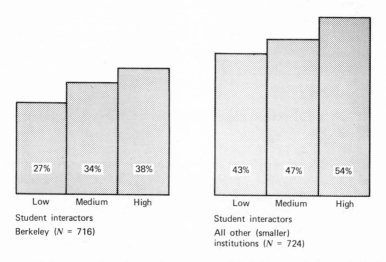

Figure 3.   Percentage of students who as seniors felt that more than one-half of the faculty at their institutions were really interested in students and their problems, by amount of out-of-class interaction reported with faculty and institution attended.

stitutions are the most striking. While high-interacting students at all institutions tended to sense greater faculty concern for students than did students whose interaction experiences were minimal, at Berkeley high-interactors felt that fewer faculty were really interested in students than did even the least frequent interactors at the other institutions combined. Only 38 percent of the Berkeley high-interactors felt that more than one-half of the faculty was really interested in students and their problems, whereas 54 percent of the high-interactors and 43 percent of the low-interactors elsewhere felt that same proportion of faculty to be really interested.

Were these Berkeley students right? Are most Berkeley faculty members in fact not only less interactive with students outside the classroom, but also less interested in students generally? Are they less committed to undergraduate teaching? Do they try less hard to communicate with or to reach their students?

As might be expected from the diversity of institutions included in the study, there is considerable variation among the institutions in the extent of their faculties' commitment to undergraduate teaching. While 71 percent of all faculty in the study expressed a preference for teaching over engaging in research, at Berkeley faculty were about evenly divided in their preferences for these activities—51 percent preferring research, 49 percent preferring teaching. Both teaching and research are, of course, not only esteemed by but expected of Berkeley faculty. Santa Cruz also had a substantial percentage (42 percent) of faculty who preferred research, even though that campus was begun with a major commitment to undergraduate education. The Luther faculty, on the other hand, was the most unanimously committed to teaching as the preferred activity: 89 percent of the Luther faculty indicated that for them teaching was the most enjoyable of the two activities. At Luther, of course, research finds little material support and is neither expected nor as greatly esteemed as it is at the University of California. At each of the other institutions about one-fifth of the faculty preferred research to teaching, even though these institutions vary in the extent to which research is institutionally supported. Stated in positive terms, about four out of five teachers in these other institutions preferred teaching, compared to nine out of ten at Luther and only one out of two at Berkeley.

Not all faculty who enjoy teaching, however, are as equally committed to undergraduate teaching as they are to the training of graduate students. Again, institutional variation is considerable. About one out of every two Berkeley faculty in the sample expressed a preference for teaching graduate students and almost as many—45 percent—of the faculty at Northeastern Illinois State College also would prefer graduate to undergraduate teaching. At Monteith and at the University of the Pacific, about one out of every three faculty members would prefer graduate instruction. Even at Santa Cruz, where the number of graduate students has been limited, a little more than one out of every four teachers would prefer to teach graduate students. At Clark, Luther, and Shimer—institutions where there are no graduate training programs—there were few faculty misfits in that between 84 and 89 percent of the faculty preferred the type of teaching they were hired to do—that is, the teaching of undergraduates.

There are institutional differences, too, in the teaching styles employed by faculty inside the classroom and in the extent to which faculty attempt to reach out to students, to communicate with them about contemporary issues. Berkeley faculty, for example, less often encourage student participation in the conduct of their classes; they less often invite students to help make class plans or policy, ask for student evaluation of courses, or give students responsibility for presenting topics, conducting panels or leading class discussions—all items in the *Student Participation* scale. Whereas only 14 percent of the Berkeley faculty scored high on this scale, 31 percent of the faculty at the other seven institutions did so. It has already been noted that Berkeley students spoke out less often in their favorite classes; no doubt there is a connection between the encouragement of student participation and the actual participation of students in class discussion. Unfortunately, data was not collected on class size—either from the students or from the faculty—but it must be presumed that some of the depressed Berkeley scores are due to the overall larger class sizes at the University. Given the uniqueness of Berkeley teaching and learning experiences on so many variables, however, it is unlikely that class size—any more than total institutional size—accounts for all of the differences in teaching and learning behaviors of faculty and students.

On another teaching scale, *Presentation Interest,* Berkeley faculty also scored lower than faculty elsewhere. Fully 49 percent of the Berkeley faculty scored low on this scale, compared to 32 percent of the faculty elsewhere; only 21 percent of the Berkeley faculty rated themselves high, whereas 29 percent of the other faculties combined did so. Yet this teaching scale, unlike the *Student Participation* scale, consists of teaching practices that do not depend on small class size for their enactment. Indeed, in many ways, the practices that make up the scale are ideally suited to the large lecture class where it is the teacher, rather than the students, who is decidedly stage center.

Berkeley faculty differed much less from faculty elsewhere in the extent to which they talked with students about issues of contemporary importance, such as drugs or the draft. Still, the comparison is interesting if only because Berkeley students in many ways were in the vanguard of the counterculture and anti-war movements. For that reason one might expect that Berkeley faculty would have the greatest experience in discussing such issues with students.* Yet only 30 percent of the Berkeley teachers scored high on a *Discussing Youth Culture Issues* scale, compared to 38 percent of the faculty elsewhere.

Regarding nearly every one of the teaching and learning experiences this study has shown to be effective, great numbers of faculty and students were found to be in some measure short-changing both themselves and each other. While this was generally true everywhere, it was most true of Berkeley. Berkeley faculty appear to neglect their undergraduate students by their greater indifference to undergraduate education and their preference for research and graduate training, for which they have attained great renown. Probably because these competing activities claim much time and energy Berkeley faculty are unable to make themselves available to undergraduate students both inside and outside the classroom. But Berkeley undergraduates seem to contribute to this situation themselves; they less often take active roles in their own education by seeking out especially meaningful learning experiences and taking part in exchanges with their teachers both inside and outside the classroom. Undoubtedly there are environmental factors at work that impede the kinds of teaching and learning experiences which this study has found to be effective. Not all of the impediments to effective teaching and learning arise out of the wishes and habits of faculty and students. There are policies and procedures, organizational structures, and competing demands on faculty that also contribute. What some of these may be and how they might be changed are discussed in the next chapter.

* Teaching assistants were not included in the sample. At Berkeley, it may well be that it is the teaching assistants who have the closest contact with students.

Chapter 16

Increasing the Effectiveness of Undergraduate Learning and Teaching

Thus far the findings that have emerged from this study have been presented as relatively separate and isolated panels of a mosaic depicting some of the ways in which students and faculty of a variety of institutions pursue learning and teaching. Relationships among some of the major components—the interests and goals of students and faculty, modes of learning and teaching, and types of change or impact—have revealed a variety of patterns and designs, some unique, others recurrent. In this chapter we assemble the sections of the mosaic and observe the finished work in terms of the original purposes of the study, and examine its practical implications for increasing the effectiveness of undergraduate learning and teaching, particularly those kinds of learning and teaching that make a difference in the lives of students.

At the most general level, four conclusions may be drawn. First, this study indicates that faculty members do make a difference in the lives of students. Indeed, they appear to have even more impact than was indicated by the earlier research summarized by Jacob (1957) and by Feldman and Newcomb (1969). This earlier research consisted primarily of data obtained only from students. Evidence in this study was derived from students at the beginning and the end of their college careers as well as from faculty members; analyses within and between these multiple data sources revealed the importance of teachers to student development. Most students named teachers of stimulating courses and teachers who had contributed to their development, and most of the students said the teachers were helpful in a variety of specific ways. Most of the faculty thought that they exerted at least some influence on students with whom they came into contact and named specific individuals to whom they felt they had contributed a great deal.

Second, the study revealed that some students made better use of their teachers than others. Students who reported changing the most and who showed actual increases in intellectual orientation had greater amounts of interaction with the faculty. The amount of faculty–student interaction beyond the classroom, in particular, was correlated with a number of reported benefits and measured changes. Although the interests and activities students pursue in college is largely determined by the characteristics they bring with them to college, their subsequent experiences with teachers play a major role in what they get out of college. In fact, even when entering characteristics were held constant, the amount and quality of interaction with faculty members, both in and out of class, were positively related to intellectual development.

Third, some faculty members are more effective than others. There is a distinctive configuration of factors characterizing teachers who have the greatest impact on students. The important role of interaction with students beyond the classroom has shown up repeatedly, and such interaction brings significant benefits to faculty members as well as to students.

Finally, some environments are more successful in creating the conditions that bring students and faculty together in productive relationships than are others. In particular, small colleges that stress undergraduate education provide a more nurturant setting for the intellectual and personal encounters between student and faculty shown to be related to student growth than do large universities with strong research missions. Subcolleges, which clustered like-minded students and faculty in a supportive environment, created the conditions of impact better than the larger, undifferentiated parts of the same universities.

In the remainder of this chapter the specific factors associated with effective learning, effective teaching, and effective milieus will be summarized, and several implications of these factors for improving the quality of undergraduate education will be explored.

EFFECTIVE LEARNING

The study has revealed a number of findings that have implications for improving the effectiveness of undergraduate learning. One of the most significant findings was the great variability that exists among students. Students direct their interests and activities in very different ways, have different learning styles, and interact in various patterns with their teachers (Chapter 11). Even among the serious students, college involvements seem to take different forms. On one hand, the vocationally and academically oriented students assiduously pursue a largely prescribed program of studies, spend long hours studying, and regard most extracurricular activities—including those of an intellectual or cultural nature—as a waste of time. These students seem to have little time for interacting with faculty or peers, and the major reward they seem to reap for their efforts is a high grade point average and a vocational direction.

On the other hand, the intellectual, artistic, and activist students take a broader view of education. While they do not shun studying, and do not emerge from college with low grade point averages, neither of these concerns seems to be as important to them as they are to those who are more academically and vocationally oriented. These students favor independent study over taking established courses and are the most likely to initiate new courses in order to see that their own intellectual interests and needs are met by their institutions. Theirs are the voices in the classroom; they more frequently speak out both in and out of their classes, and for that reason they probably wield disproportionate influence on the thinking of faculty members when they design courses, prepare lectures, or make up examinations. In addition, these are the students who interact most with faculty members outside the classroom and to whom other students turn for information about courses or instructors. It would appear, therefore, that different kinds of students profit from different kinds of learning experiences.

Particularly important for the development of all kinds of students, however, is an opportunity for continuing interaction with faculty members. Those students who have had the most interaction with faculty members outside of class, however limited that may be in absolute terms, have gained more educational benefits than those who have had the least interaction (Chapter 11). Although there is evidence that students with different interests talk about different topics, most seem to thrive on this kind of experience with faculty. The most educationally significant encounters between students and their teachers were the result of close, broad, and continuous relationships (Chapter 12). Further, the amount of faculty–student interaction was positively related to the amount of increase in intellectual orientation, which embraced both broadening intrinsic intellectual interests and increasing personal openness, cognitive complexity, and flexibility to explore them (Chapter 13). Clearly, there is a need to facilitate these kinds of effective relationships in and out of class.

A third recurrent theme has been the students' aggressive use of the environment and their active role in their own education. The extent of student use of the institution, particularly the faculty, was related to their self-perceived cognitive and affective growth (Chapter 11) and to measured changes in intellectual disposition (Chapter 13). Although students cannot derive benefits from a barren environment, neither can a rich environment have much impact unless students put forth considerable effort themselves and assume the major share of responsibility for educating themselves.

Although much of what makes a difference in the growth of students has to do with nonclassroom factors, classes, too, have an important role to play. As was seen in Chapter 12, when a student takes two or more courses from the same faculty member, that becomes a potent device for creating a continuing relationship. But some courses seem more facilitative of student growth than others; those that make connections with the affective life, relate to student concerns, and involve readings which stir the imagination are more likely to facilitate the growth and development of students.

Finally, the role of values has been touched upon several times. Although students described the faculty member who contributed most to their development as having stimulated them intellectually, a large number indicated that the faculty member also increased their awareness of social issues and their own values (Chapter 12). Further, students who became more intellectually disposed were more likely to be striving to expand their self-awareness (Chapter 13), and those faculty members who were most effective had discussed value-laden youth culture issues with students (Chapter 10). Educational programs that extend beyond cognitive rationality and encourage the discussion of values and controversial issues, this evidence indicates, would be more likely to have a significant impact on the lives of students.

These findings regarding the key characteristics of students who learn different lessons to different degrees from their teachers have implications for the improvement of college learning. First, although students vary and each must seek improvement in ways based upon his own unique history, all might benefit by confronting several questions about themselves that are raised by this study:

- How committed to learning within the context of colleges and universities are you, and do you make a major investment of time and energy in learning those things which will likely be of long-term value to you?

- Do you try to communicate your major concerns to your teachers so that they may respond to them in class?
- Do you assume your share of the responsibility to encounter the course content, to participate in class discussions, and to make the classroom experience interesting to both your peers and your teachers?
- How often do you try to extend the classroom by pursuing ideas and issues with teachers and other students outside of class?
- Do you try to relate course content to your own personal experiences and to see their implications for social problems and issues?
- How are you growing and developing as a person?
- Are you getting all you can from your college experience?

Unfortunately, students by and large are not likely to confront questions such as these. Students are seldom asked by faculty members to discuss educational issues in classes—which is curious, given their centrality to the educational process—and they are not common topics of discussion among most peer groups. Outside of occasional orientation sessions for freshmen, which seldom force students to grapple with serious educational issues, there are no institutionally ordained times when students are urged to consider issues such as these. Thus, faculty members and administrators should make special efforts to raise these questions with students and, because they admit of no final answers, raise them again and again throughout the students' college careers.

The findings also have implications for educational policies and procedures that may improve the effectiveness of learning among students. In particular, they indicate the need to individualize instruction, expand learning options, reorganize and perhaps redefine general education, and emphasize values.

Individualizing Instruction   The great diversity among students is a major reason why attention should be given to individualizing the learning experiences and tailoring them as much as possible to each student. It is a classic pedagogical problem, of course, to reconcile the learning needs of individuals with those of a group and of the subject, and there are not likely to be permanent solutions. However, a number of current efforts appear to be promising.

One form of individualized instruction, variously known as self-paced learning, mastery learning, personalized system of instruction

(PSI), and the Keller Plan (after one of the early proponents of this approach), has been used in literally hundreds of colleges and universities and in the full range of academic disciplines. In his seminal paper, "Goodbye Teacher," Keller (1968) set forth his instructional plan as having five characteristics that distinguish it from conventional lecture and discussion approaches. It is an individually-paced, mastery-oriented, student-tutored course that relies on study guides to communicate information to students and involves only a few lectures by teachers for the specific purpose of motivating and stimulating students. The entire course is divided into several units, and the students proceed through the units in the prescribed sequence; however, they are not allowed to continue to the next unit until they are able to master almost perfectly the material in the current unit. The instructor chooses and plans the course content, writes the study guides, and prepares the examinations following each unit. The tutor grades the examinations and helps students who may need some assistance learning a unit. A rather extensive literature on the evaluation of these kinds of courses has appeared, and a review of the studies reaches the following conclusions (Kulik, Kulik, & Carmichael, 1974, p. 383).

1. The Keller Plan is a very attractive teaching method to most students. In every published report, students rate the Keller Plan more favorably than teaching by lecture.
2. Self-pacing and interaction with tutors seem to be the features of the Keller courses most favored by students.
3. Several investigators report higher-than-average withdrawal rates for their Keller sections. The conditions that influence withdrawal and procrastination in Keller courses have been studied, and it seems possible to control procrastination and withdrawal through course design.
4. Content learning (as measured by final examinations) is adequate in Keller courses. In the published studies, final examination performance in Keller sections always equals, and usually exceeds, performance in lecture sections.
5. Students almost invariably report that they learn more in PSI than in lecture courses, and also nearly always report putting more time and effort into the Keller courses.

The evidence compiled thus far constitutes a fine recommendation for individualized instruction, at least as a portion of a student's experience.

For those persons who believe the above approach is so tightly structured that students do not have room enough to achieve different learning goals, a course or curricular contract may be a more appealing device. The basic idea behind the course contract is that each student in concert with a teacher prepares a set of learning goals, the learning experiences he will obtain to achieve those goals, and the criteria by which he will be evaluated. When the contract is agreed upon by the student and the teacher, it becomes a binding agreement. Several schools have extended this concept to apply to a student's entire college curriculum. For example, at Ottawa University in Kansas and Evergreen State College in Washington students plan their entire curricula with the assistance of a small faculty committee. The curriculum may draw from the resources of the entire school and community and it may consist of regular courses, independent readings, special seminars, and related on- and off-campus activities. Not only does this approach allow courses and curricula to bend to meet the specific needs of individual students, it also has the advantage of placing a large part of the responsibility for students' education squarely on their shoulders, thereby assuring that they become actively involved in planning, executing, and evaluating their own education.

There are times, however, when students will have to be treated as a part of a group, sometimes a large group. How can a teacher individualize a course with a large enrollment? This is a difficult problem, but there are a number of techniques to cope with it. Multiple option courses are one device. Here students may choose among several options by which they may achieve the learning objectives of a course. Or some courses may have multiple objectives, and students may decide which objectives would be most consonant with their interests and plans. Martin Covington at Berkeley has been using this multiple option approach in his psychology courses.

Another technique is a computer-assisted teaching tool which has been developed by Allen Kelley at the University of Wisconsin. Called the Teaching Information Processing System (TIPS), it is a procedure for obtaining feedback about student progress and responding to their individual needs. Every week or two each student is asked to complete a brief multiple choice "survey" designed to measure his understanding of basic concepts. The testing is not used for grading purposes but to diagnose difficulties so that students may be helped before the examinations are given. Within a few hours three separate computer printouts may be available, one for each student, one for each teaching assistant, and one for the professor. According to a description of this procedure the student report not only tells each person how well he did, but they

> ... recall weaknesses revealed in earlier surveys, suggest ways in which past and present deficiencies might best be overcome, and lay out individually tailored assignments for the period immediately ahead. . . . A learner who has performed well may receive an optional assignment or required work at a higher level for extra course credit. A student who has demonstrated a lack of understanding of one particular concept is likely to be assigned work specifically calculated to overcome that shortcoming. A student whose performance has been consistently poor may be asked to attend review sessions, while a student whose performance has been outstanding may be offered the option of undertaking a special project or tutoring low-achieving students in lieu of taking a midterm examination. (Freymann, 1973, p. 2)

The reports to the teaching assistant summarize the progress of students in their sections, and the report to the professor is a composite of all student reports.

Expanding Learning Options   In most institutions of higher learning, whether university or community college, public or private, large or small, learning is organized in similar ways. Most instruction is conducted on a college *campus*, within the framework of an academic *department*, and in a *classroom*, even though many students as well as teachers are able to derive substantial learning off-campus, in interdisciplinary programs, and outside the classroom. In order to capitalize on the wide variation in learning styles among students and the learning opportunities in other settings, the range of acceptable and legitimate learning and teaching experiences should be extended far beyond what is commonplace in most institutions today.

Partly as a response to the student pressures of the 1960s there is somewhat more opportunity for students to learn in settings other than the campus. New institutions such as Empire State College and Minnesota Metropolitan State College and new external degree programs such as the Consortium organized within the California State University and Colleges, illustrate one major contemporary thrust to "take education to where the people are."

Other off-campus experiences are provided as adjuncts to a campus-based program. These learning experiences take several forms:

- Field trips to community agencies, jails, drug-treatment programs, and government offices to illustrate issues in connection with individual courses.

- Internships in which students spend some time working in an agency or organization and observing how the organization, the staff, and the clients function.
- Work-study programs in which students combine academic and vocational experiences. Some of these follow the Antioch plan of alternating periods of full-time work and full-time study, and others follow the Berea plan in which students engage in work and study at the same time.
- Semester away plans in which a student spends a semester in such enriching places as Washington, D.C., New York, at the United Nations, or an overseas campus, receives instruction and obtains credit for the experience.
- Foreign travel.

Increasingly, educators are coming to realize that these off-campus experiences play a valuable role in broadening students' experience, raising intellectual questions for them to pursue, applying concepts learned in the classroom, increasing motivation for study, and generally addressing that classical pedagogical challenge of bridging the gulf between academic and non-academic experiences.

Although it is apparent that these experiences *may* connect with the classroom work of students, it also happens that they often do *not*. The College of Community Studies at Northwestern University under the leadership of David Epperson is in the process of developing and testing various "action-reflection models" of education. Although the results are not yet in, this school has initiated an intriguing programmatic effort to send students off-campus for experiences in local agencies, distant cities, and foreign countries; emphasize combinations of individual and group work; and include an academic component to supplement the experiential. The evaluative research, which is conducted largely by doctoral students, attempts to determine the learning outcomes of these different procedures. This effort should provide useful information to others who are trying to extend learning opportunities beyond the campus and yet make those experiences relate to the concepts, theories, and methods studied on the campus.

But on-campus learning opportunities may be expanded too. Interdisciplinary courses and programs that focus on contemporary social problems, and on intellectual themes, are of interest to many young men and women. Although schools do not prohibit such courses and programs, the fact that faculty members typically are hired, paid, and advanced through departments makes it difficult for them to initiate and sustain such efforts, especially during this time of fiscal retrenchment. Separate offices charged with providing assistance and support to students or to faculty members who wish to study these issues have been found to be useful organizational devices to facilitate these kinds of courses at a number of schools.

Extra-classroom learning is also an important way of broadening traditional approaches. Independent study, tutorials, and individual reading courses are valuable alternatives to classroom lectures and discussions for some of the students all of the time and for all of the students some of the time. Audio-tutorial approaches have utility, particularly for mastering basic details of a field of study, such as foreign language and some of the sciences. Conducting research and writing scholarly papers is a valuable learning experience for many; at the University of California, Santa Cruz, it has been reported (McHenry, 1973) that the proportion of graduates who chose to write theses has increased from nine percent in 1968–69 to 20 percent in 1969–70, 31 percent in 1970–71, and 45 percent in 1971–72.

These extensions of the range of learning opportunities not only attempt to meet the needs of different students but to help them make closer connections between their work in the classroom and the realities in the larger world.

Reorganize General Education College students generally are expected to acquire a broad general education as well as a mastery of some specialized body of knowledge. The primary way these goals are implemented is to require students to take at least one course in several different academic disciplines, usually general survey, and several courses in one field. Yet, it is questionable whether this conventional arrangement provides the broad liberal outlook so often promised by colleges and universities. Only about half of the students in this sample increased their intellectual disposition, which includes broadening intellectual interests and becoming open to new ideas, during their entire four-year college career. Also, seniors who were asked to name the course that had been the most stimulating in terms of subject matter, perspective, or ideas, virtually never mentioned survey courses, although ostensibly they are supposed to serve that purpose.

The reasons for the neglect of general education are not hard to detect. General education courses are under the direction and control of the several academic departments, most of which have a more vital interest in providing specialized education for their "majors." It is a nearly universal practice to have a higher student–teacher ratio for lower division introductory courses than for the upper division specialized courses; introductory courses generally utilize less popular lecture teaching techniques than the advanced courses; and because faculty members tend to regard introductory courses as a less desirable assignment, teachers of these courses tend to be less capable or more reluctant than others. It is perhaps poetic justice that recently several departments have suffered from their past neglect of general education courses when course requirements in their fields have been dropped, and students sought more interesting work elsewhere; indeed, some of the loss of faculty jobs in less popular subjects can be traced to this cause.

What can be done? Clearly there are no simple solutions to such a complex issue. Five Washington-based higher education associations under the leadership of the American Association of Colleges have embarked on a five-year, multimillion dollar project to develop and field test new models of undergraduate liberal education. Such a massive effort is proportional to the magnitude of the task. However, a few promising directions for such reform may be mentioned in the following paragraphs.

First, there is a need to recognize that the present reliance on introductory survey courses of the academic disciplines in most instances does not introduce students to significant new ideas, perspectives, or issues. The fact that students often don't want to take them and faculty members often don't want to teach them is testimony to their educational barrenness.

But what can be put in their place? One possibility would be to replace survey courses that try to cover briefly all major subdivisions of a discipline with disciplinary offerings with more highly focused content. By making these courses "perspectives in" rather than "surveys of" the disciplines, teachers might be freed from their real or imagined need to "cover the field." They could then concentrate their time and attention on helping students understand a few of the dominant perspectives in the field, become familiar with a few of the major thinkers and their works, and acquire some of the key concepts. This approach, though on the surface similar to existing practice, would provide an opportunity for students to get deeply enough involved in a discipline that they can gain an appreciation of its distinctive way of understanding the world and its place in the spectrum of human knowledge.

A different approach would be to replace surveys with courses that are organized around important social and personal issues. Freshman seminars, taught by excellent teachers, were introduced by Harvard, Stanford, and countless other institutions during the 1960s, and this suggestion is a natural extension of that approach. Lower division seminars could deal with timely and relevant issues, and could provide a testing ground to see what the various disciplines can offer to the understanding of the various issues. As the recent years have demonstrated, often scholars and their disciplines have had relatively little to contribute toward the solution of several serious social problems. The interplay between the needs of the problem or issue and the contributions of the disciplines toward an intellectual solution of the problem could provide students with an opportunity to test out the value of several disciplines, stimulate teachers to explore the interstices between their fields and the "real" world, and perhaps stimulate new research or communication of research in the disciplines. The Successful Freshman Exploratory Program at the University of Redlands as well as Berkeley's new Strawberry Creek College seminar program established by Charles Muscatine, have adopted variations of this model of lower division instruction.

A different approach would be to turn the general and specialized education around, allow a student to begin working on his major interests as soon as he begins college and develop general courses that build from and enrich his specialization. This technique would allow students to get deeply involved in their "majors" during their first two years, and as has been characteristic of European universities, develop ancillary competencies as they realize they are needed. Franconia College in Vermont has adopted this approach.

The major point to be made here is not that any one of these alternative approaches is the answer, but that they illustrate various ways individual colleges and universities may go about reconceptualizing how to provide a general education with substance and excitement for students. Evidence from this study, although not definitive, supports the critics of liberal learning as it is practiced today, and does indicate that schools will have to find new ways to realize their lofty goals and to utilize their human and fiscal resources.

Emphasize Values   The role of values has arisen repeatedly in this study. The most effective faculty members often discussed value-laden issues such as sex, the war, and alternative life styles with students, and students who became most intellectually disposed had shown the greatest interest in expanding their self-awareness and had been involved in some of the controversial activities of the day. These findings are strikingly consistent with the conclusion reached by Jacob (1957, p. 8).

> ... the impetus to change does not come primarily from the formal educational process. Potency to affect student values is found in the distinctive climate of a few institutions, the individual and personal magnetism of a sensitive teacher with strong value-commitments of his own, or value-laden personal experiences of students imaginatively integrated with their intellectual development.

Yet, the long-term trend toward secularization in higher education and the ascendancy of public higher education over the private, often church-related, colleges has accompanied the decline of values in academia. Consideration of issues of choice and purpose and speculation about what might be are viewed as value judgments, and as such have come to be regarded as outside the realm of legitimate scholarly attention. In this context it is hard to justify efforts to help students learn to formulate ethical standards, participate in the body politic, invent their futures, develop new forms of self-expression, and create community. The upheavals on the campuses during the 1960s may be seen, at least in part, as the attempt by many students and faculty members to come to grips with vital value questions that had been largely ignored in the academic world.

It is time to recognize that there is no such thing as a value-free education. Rather than deny that values are involved, educators might better affirm that values as well as facts are part of education; then they could consider ways to help students become aware of values, learn to critically analyze value judgments, develop a respect for diverse value positions, and elaborate a value scheme that may guide their lives. This does not mean indoctrination, or the imposition of any particular moral code. But it does mean helping students develop sensitivity and awareness about values, purposes, and choices in human life.

How can this awareness be fostered? One of the authors taught a course for freshmen designed to help them confront some of the issues facing an individual in a democracy. The course was divided into several units, each dealing with a different set of issues, such as political theory of democracy, economic assumptions in capitalism and other economies, alienation in modern life, and the ideal of equality of opportunity. Booklets containing classical and contemporary writings on each subject were prepared, and they served as the basic reading. Although there were a few lectures, mainly by social analysts and critics, the heart of the course consisted of small group seminars led by teaching assistants. These seminars were not designed to treat all the issues involved in each topic but instead to allow a vigorous discussion of many of the most controversial issues. Evaluations over a period of years indicated that this was a moving educational experience for most of the students; indeed, it was one of the few programs Jacob was able to find that had demonstrable impact on the value outcomes of students. Similar courses could easily become a part of the general education of students and help them become attuned to values in their lives and in the society.

Virtually all of the professions have lost much of the confidence of the people in recent years, and all could respond to the current situation by having their students take courses on topical and controversial issues facing the profession. Medical students need to explore the transplant issues, the ethics of prolonging the lives of individuals with no hope of recovery, and the equitable distribution of medical care. Engineering students need to consider the purposes to which their work may be put, and the legal profession might develop educational programs that would help it avoid a future Watergate debacle. Courses that explore the enduring as well as topical value questions confronting the profession would seem to be a valuable part of professional education today, and could help broaden the thinking and perspectives of future practitioners.

Another possibility would be for students to learn about the lives of scholars, about their personal experienes, their conflicts, and the ways they went about making critical decisions in their lives. The study of lives of major intellectual figures has seldom occurred, most academics being more concerned with the ideas, theories, and methodologies advanced by individuals independently of other aspects of the persons. The result is a kind of naivete among students regarding the lives of intellectuals, as though their ideas burst forth independent of the person. Books like the *Double Helix*, which describe the human beings involved in scientific and scholarly work in all of their frailty and complexity would allow students to have a more realistic view of the academic world and also see how others have coped with values and made critical choices in their lives.

Traditionally the humanities have been the disciplines that have dealt with the value and humane dimensions of human existence and helped students to develop a richer inner life and social conscience. However, humanistic faculty members have alternately been intimidated and impressed by the power of the scientific methods and increasingly have sought to emulate them. As a result, they have neglected some of their traditional liberal education functions. There is a need to find ways to strengthen and reinvigorate these disciplines so that they can once again help college students to examine their values and enrich their inner lives.

Several years ago there was a flurry of activity to develop science courses for nonscience students, courses that were designed to help students appreciate the nature and power of the scientific methods. It may be appropriate to design courses on humanistic perspectives in natural and social sciences that would help students in these specialties to examine value and humane aspects of those fields. In this way students who may otherwise regard the study of humanities as an irrelevant detour in their educational career, may become sensitive to humanistic views within the context of their major concerns.

In summary, it would seem that colleges and universities might facilitate the kinds of learning associated with changes in the lives of students by individualizing instruction, expanding learning opportunities, reorganizing general education, and emphasizing values.

EFFECTIVE TEACHING

Effective faculty members do not perfunctorily enact their roles as undergraduate teachers. They more often go beyond their prescribed task of transmitting knowledge and skills to students than do their colleagues. They are more committed to teaching, especially to teaching undergraduates, and in their classrooms they work harder at stimulating student interest in the content of the courses they teach. They more often exchange ideas with students regarding current social, political, and cultural issues and changes in the society at large. In this way they both respond to student desires for greater social relevance in their education and relate to students as partners in the learning enterprise. Moreover, the attempts of effective teachers to stimulate, to relate, and to educate are not limited to their classroom activities: they more frequently interact with students beyond the classroom as well, discussing careers and educational plans, course-related ideas, campus issues, and problems of immediate personal concern to individual students (Chapter 10).

Effective teachers were most frequently described as being available and open to any discussion by the students who named them as having contributed the most to their educational and/or personal development (Chapter 12). Faculty who experienced the most frequent interaction with students outside the classroom were also both more often physically available—by keeping office hours and frequenting student gathering places, lounges or cafeterias—and psychologically accessible—by being more student-oriented both in attitude and in the conduct of their classes (Chapter 6).

Teachers, at least those concerned with more than mastery of cognitive knowledge, seem to be most effective when they establish relatively close, friendly relationships with students over a substantial period of time. The most significant faculty–student relationships were seldom described by faculty as impersonal, and almost all such relationships were associated with continuing faculty–student interaction (Chapter 12). Nevertheless, teachers who were more accessible and more interactive with students were not merely being friendly or gregarious; they exerted considerable intellectual impact as well. Most students described the faculty members who contributed most to them as having stimulated them intellectually, demanded high quality work of them, made them feel confident of their own abilities, and interested them in the teachers' fields (Chapters 12 and 13). Furthermore, these interactive factors were characteristic of intellectually influential faculty who were said to have contributed to students who actually became more intellectually disposed.

It appears that in a variety of ways the most effective faculty communicate to students their desire to be effective as teachers and to be of service to students in pursuit of their own goals. Some effective faculty were more helpful with vocational goals, others with questions of personal or social values, still others with more strictly academic or intellectual goals (Chapters 12 and 13). Yet all showed a similar willingness to listen, to discuss and, if possible, to help. No doubt there are factors in addition to those included in this study that affect a teacher's ability to have impact on students, but that is a question which further and different kinds of research might profitably address.

Such findings regarding the salient characteristics of teachers who affect the lives of students have many implications for the improvement of college teaching. Although faculty members vary in their styles and therefore each must seek improvement in his own way, all teachers could benefit by asking themselves questions such as the following that have been raised by this study:

- To what extent are you aware of the diversity of student interests that exists in your classes? What are you doing to relate the course content to those various concerns?

- Is your teaching style uniform or do you employ a variety of techniques depending on the nature of the students, the course material, or the teaching setting?
- What kinds of oral and visual presentation techniques do you use to stimulate student interest in course materials?
- How do you go about conveying your enthusiasm for teaching to your students and colleagues? Do you discuss teaching and learning issues with your students and colleagues?
- Do you know who the *best* teachers are in your own department or school? The *worst* teachers? Have you ever observed their teaching? Upon what other kinds of evidence do you base your feelings that these are the best or worst teachers?
- Do you try to overcome the natural barriers between students and faculty? How do you go about indicating your accessibility to students?
- How effectively do you use casual and informal conversations with students outside the classroom as a vehicle for teaching?

Unfortunately, in the past most college and university professors have not been required to confront these kinds of questions. Although they are usually well-educated in their academic disciplines, few faculty members receive any kind of training or preparation for college teaching. And once hired, few faculty ever receive any in-service training or indeed any assistance at all in learning to teach.

There is some evidence, however, that this situation is changing. With student enrollments leveling off, many institutions are finding themselves "tenured in" and are seeking ways to provide staff flexibility. At one institution in this study 79 percent of the faculty have tenure; at another of these schools 63 percent of the faculty are scheduled to retire after the year 2000. Both institutions must find ways to stimulate the professional and personal renewal of its existing faculty over the coming decades. The tight labor market is affecting individuals, too; faculty members are finding it harder to find jobs, change jobs, or even gain tenure at their own institutions. Thus, many individual faculty members and a number of colleges and universities are actively supporting in-service training programs, particularly those that aim to help faculty members grow and develop in their roles as teachers. Because these programs were discussed in Study I, they will not be repeated here. Suffice it to say that the various proposals made in Chapter 8 for developing innovative teaching strategies, evaluating teaching, and creating programs to help faculty members develop their teaching styles, hold promise for improving teaching.

EFFECTIVE MILIEUS

Students and faculty meet within the context of a social milieu, and the effectiveness of even the best learners and teachers depends on the environment within which they function. Consistent with previous findings, this study repeatedly revealed the importance of the quality of faculty–student interaction both in and out of class for realizing educational benefits for both students and faculty members. Chapter 15 indicated that the quality of such interaction varies among different kinds of institutions.

Specifically, Berkeley faculty are more inclined to prefer research to teaching and graduate to undergraduate teaching, have less favorable attitudes toward personal interaction with students, and are less available to undergraduates than are faculty at the other schools. And students there have less interaction with faculty members both in and out of class. Furthermore, those students who have become more intellectually disposed have had to be even more aggressive in seeking out faculty than students who have changed similarly in other institutions (Chapter 13).

Since the time of this study, however, there are a number of signs that this too may be changing. Recent actions by the California State Legislature, the Board of Regents, and the administration which were mentioned in Chapter 8 suggest a renewed concern with undergraduate instruction at Berkeley. Furthermore, the growth of training programs for teaching assistants and the innovative restructuring of many undergraduate courses on the Berkeley campus in recent years is testimony to the fact that many faculty members do care and that given the proper kinds of institutional support they will undertake to improve the quality of undergraduate teaching and learning.

Furthermore, Berkeley is widely recognized as a renowned center for scholarly research and graduate and professional education. It has managed to retain this distinction even in the face of political criticism and fiscal constraints suffered in recent years. Since faculty members cannot be all things to all people, their commitment to excellence in other areas makes it difficult to devote themselves with equal energy to undergraduate education.

At the other end of the continuum, small residential colleges, where close faculty–student relations are part of their tradition and image, were more likely to foster greater interaction. There is also evidence that cluster colleges at the University of the Pacific and at Santa Cruz have succeeded in promoting greater interaction among more students and faculty, with consequent benefits to each. Yet, even in these more favorable settings, large numbers of both students and teachers have chosen to remain within their own spheres.

These findings have several implications for improving the climate for teaching and learning with particular relevance for nontraditional learning programs, institutional missions, and cluster colleges.

Recently, such nontraditional programs as the university-without-walls, sponsored by the Union for Experimenting Colleges and Universities, and the external-degree programs, offered by Empire State College in the State University of New York system, have attracted national attention. Their potential to provide new ways of going to college and to make college accessible to many who desire and deserve further education is considerable, and such programs deserve the interest and support they have received.

Yet data from this study indicate that students and teachers derive many benefits from close and continuous interaction. Although levels of such interaction are not particularly high for campus-based programs, the opportunity for such interaction is likely to be far more limited in off-campus programs. Designers of new ventures in off-campus learning should recognize the demonstrated importance of personal interaction of teacher and student and take special steps to maximize it. Unless there are definite structures to support such contact in the absence of a campus, these new ventures may well provide no greater educational benefits than correspondence courses. Alternative structures to reach new students are needed, but at the heart of an educational experience is the relationship between teacher and learner, and the best educational setting helps realize the potential in that relationship.

The American university historically has attempted to perform three very different purposes: conduct scholarly research, educate graduate students, and educate undergraduate students. The relationships between these purposes have always been characterized by a dynamic of uneasy tension. More often than not, undergraduate education suffers at the hands of the other two.

This does not mean that an institution may not find ways to combine all three missions in a balanced way. Nor should it be taken to mean that maor universities should sacrifice research and advanced education in favor of undergraduate education, for the nation requires both. But if an institution with heavy commitments in scholarship and graduate education does offer an undergraduate program, it ought not sacrifice its undergraduate students to those other missions. And if it truly seeks excellence in each area, it may well have to establish special organizational supports for its undergraduate program.

Small, semiautonomous subcolleges have been established not merely by major universities but by a wide variety of large or growing institutions to provide more supportive environments for undergraduate education. Part of the basic rationale underlying the development of such schools is that they can provide the sense of community and warmer faculty–student relations characteristic of small schools and yet have the advantages and resources offered by a large and diverse institution. The findings of this study, as well as previous research (Martin, 1969; Gaff, et al., 1970), indicate that cluster colleges do in fact provide interaction between students and faculty that differs both in quality and quantity from the more traditional segments of the same institutions. Thus, there is accumulating evidence that this form of academic organization can provide a more effective educational milieu than large and monolithic institutions. Cluster colleges can enhance undergraduate programs at schools where competing missions threaten to undermine them as well as at schools with traditional commitments to undergraduate education.

However valuable cluster colleges may be for creating a supportive environment for teaching and learning, they are becoming more difficult to establish. This is because declining student enrollments make it unwise for most schools to add new units (most cluster colleges were added onto existing schools to accomodate rapid growth during the 1960s), and it is difficult politically to carve out permanent subcolleges from a large institution. Yet, it is possible to obtain close and extensive faculty–student relationships by creating less permanent educational groups. For example, Evergreen State College organizes much of its curriculum around problem-oriented groups of approximately five faculty members drawn from different disciplines and approximately 100 students. These groupings are designed to facilitate a holistic educational experience for students, with faculty members responsible for assisting both cognitive and affective development of students. These groups at Evergreen as well as at institutions that are more traditional are reported by participants to generate stimulating intellectual and personal encounters, but like other worthwhile innovative programs, to make extensive demands on them. Since this arrangement calls for faculty members to play new roles vis-à-vis their students and colleagues, these temporary groupings represent a promising feature of some newly created faculty development programs.

CONCLUSION

Modern higher education has meant for many students learning the factual content of the academic disciplines, for many faculty members the teaching of portions of cognitive knowledge, and for many institutions the efficient transmission of accumulated information. These are important traditions, and they deserve to be preserved. Many students, however, feel not only the need to learn a body of factual knowledge but also a need to acquire appreciation of the value of intellectual inquiry, increase their sensitivities and awareness, develop a personal philosophy and an outlook on life, and grow and develop as whole persons. In an effort to accomodate this diversity, many faculty members do far more than transmit the content of their academic specializations; they relate their learning to other fields of study, to realities in the larger world, and to the personal lives of students. And many colleges and universities are striving to create rich educational environments in which a wide range of learning experiences are offered, individual students and teachers are treated with regard for their unique interests and talents, and productive and humane interaction between students and teachers occurs on a regular and continuous basis.

The results of these studies provide considerable empirical evidence related to several issues involved in these views of undergraduate education. Numerous implications have been discussed that suggest ways to improve the effectiveness of learning, the effectiveness of teaching, and the effectiveness of college environments. The educational values underlying these studies are controversial, the research findings provocative, and the proposals debatable. However, the values, findings, and proposals provide general guidelines for improving undergraduate learning and teaching.

Appendix I

Table A   Numbers and Rates of Responses from Six Schools

	Sent	Returned	Rate	Analyzed
University of California, Davis	409	305	.75	303
California State University, Los Angeles	381	260	.68	257
Hofstra University	365	219	.60	210
Chabot College	179	139	.78	138
University of Puget Sound	166	131	.79	130
Bard College	59	31	.53	31
Totals	1559	1085	.70	1069

Table B   Comparison of Sample with Population Characteristics as Estimated from Two National Studies, in percentages

	1968–69 Center Study $N = 1069$	1963–64 Dunham Study $N = 138,202$	1969–70 Trow Study $N = 60,028$
Sex			
male	81	82	81
female	19	18	19
Rank			
junior	52	45	48
senior	48	51	46
other	—	4	6
Doctorate			
no	48	49	50
yes	52	51	50
Field			
humanities	23	28	23[a]
natural science	20	23	19
social science	16	15	11
professional	31	32	29
unclassified	10	6	18

[a] Major field of postgraduate degree.

DEVELOPMENT OF SCALES

For economy and efficiency in treating the data, a number of scales were derived from the questionnaire. To this end, 138 of the Likert-type variables were intercorrelated and subjected to a principal components analysis with varimax rotation (Kaiser, 1958). Eight of the components turned out to be large, interesting, and readily interpretable. Scores on the items most clearly defining the components were summed for each respondent to obtain his scale scores.

The first three scales are concerned with a faculty member's self-reported teaching practices. The remaining five scales are primarily concerned with attitudes. In Table C, the items included in each scale are listed along with their varimax loadings from the components analysis. Table D presents the intercorrelations among the derived scales. For further information on the scales and their development see Wilson, Gaff, and Bavry (1970).

The scales names and the scale numbers are:

1. Discursive Practices
2. Classroom Participation Practices
3. Evaluation Practices
4. Attitude Toward Regulation of Personal Behavior
5. Attitude Toward Personalization of Faculty–Student Interaction
6. Attitude Toward Traditional Extracurricular Activities
7. Attitude Toward Student Motivation
8. Attitude Toward Current Issues in Educational Change

Table C Teaching Practices and Attitude Scales

Item Content	Varimax[a] Loading
1. Discursive Practices	
Discuss points of view other than my own.	72
Relate the course work to other fields of study.	67
Discuss the origins of ideas introduced in the class.	62
Encourage students to discuss issues that go beyond class reading.	62
Mention reading references for points I make.	54
2. Classroom Participation Practices	
Invite students to help make class plans or policy.	68
Ask for student evaluation of the course.	55
Invite student criticism of my ideas.	53
Encourage everyone to get actively involved in the discussion.	44
Explain why I conduct the class as I do.	43
3. Evaluation Practices	
Give objective examinations.	−74
Essay examinations generally are a better measure of a student's learning than are objective tests.	73
Include examination questions for which there is no one right answer.	50
Assign term papers or projects.	39
Mark on a curve.	−39
4. Regulation of Personal Behavior	
A group of students held an anti-draft protest meeting on campus and subsequently picketed the local Selective Service Board.	76
An unmarried male and female student couple were found to be sharing the same apartment.	76
A biology teacher spoke out in his class in favor of premarital sexual relations.	74
A faculty member organized a Black Power group that engaged in some disruptive activities in the local community.	73
The student government using student funds invited a well-known social activist to the campus to speak.	70
Women's dormitories should make it possible for women to enter and leave at any time of the day or night.	70
Colleges ought to have strong rules forbidding the use of marijuana.	−70
The student newspaper carried a series of articles on the use of drugs describing in detail how to use them.	69
A faculty member participated in a nonviolent sit-in demonstration in the administration building.	68
Dress regulations have no place on a college campus.	64

Table C   (Continued)

Item Content	Varimax[a] Loading
In this day and age colleges should accord their students the freedoms and responsibilities of adults.	62
Too many students today are wrapped up in social causes.	−53
Students under 21 years of age should not be permitted to use alcohol.	−53
5. Personalization of Faculty–Student Interaction	
Informal out-of-class contacts with faculty members are an important part of a student's education.	70
It is generally best for a faculty member to go out of his way to establish friendly relations with his students.	70
Students learn class material best if a teacher takes a personal interest in them.	69
It is part of the job of a faculty member to help students with personal problems they may bring him.	60
The emotional and personal development of a student should be as important to a teacher as his intellectual development.	47
6. Traditional Extracurricular Activities	
Carnivals, parties, dances, and other campus social events usually weaken the academic program.	69
Fraternities and sororities should be barred from college campuses.	57
Usually campus extracurricular activities detract more than they add to a student's education.	54
It is generally preferable for students to participate in social improvement projects, such as tutoring children, than in campus social activities.	48
Intercollegiate athletics should be abandoned.	44
7. Student Motivation	
Students too often want to speculate on important issues before they master the relevant basic facts.	68
It is generally a better policy to help students acquire a firm foundation in the knowledge of a field before encouraging them to think about the major problems of that field.	56
Although many students are clamoring for new freedoms, few are capable of using those freedoms responsibly.	39
Without tests and grades to prod them, most students would learn little.	34
Rather than trying to relate to students as their intellectual equal, a professor should assume the role of a knowledgeable authority.	34

Table C (Continued)

Item Content	Varimax[a] Loading
8. Current Issues in Educational Change	
Increase the proportion of students from minority groups.	58
Increase the proportion of courses directed at contemporary social problems.	57
Increase the proportion of interdisciplinary courses.	55
Increase the use of independent study.	46
Students should be allowed to earn academic credit by working in community projects directly related to their academic interests.	45
Increase the amount of informal interaction between faculty and students.	41
Increase the extent to which students help to determine the content of courses.	39
Colleges should lower their formal academic admission requirements in order to accept more students from minority groups.	37

[a] Decimal omitted.

Table D Intercorrelations of Teaching Practices and Attitude Scales[a]

Scale Number	1	2	3	4	5	6	7	8
1	74							
2	41	69						
3	30	19	66					
4	14	14	33	91				
5	17	37	08	07	74			
6	07	−06	19	25	−07	62		
7	−11	−23	−27	−55	−22	−02	67	
8	20	31	32	51	33	12	−50	76

(N = 954)

[a] Decimals omitted; diagonal values are Kuder-Richardson 21 reliabilities.

Appendix II

QUESTIONNAIRE RESPONSES

Table A   Numbers and Rates of Faculty Responses

Institution	Number of Questionnaires Sent	Number of Questionnaires Returned	Response Rate
University of California:			
Berkeley	453	213	.47
Santa Cruz	214	122	.57
Northeastern Illinois State			
College	267	130	.49
Monteith College	35	19	.54
Luther College	130	89	.69
University of the Pacific	242	158	.65
Clark College	106	51	.48
Shimer College	25	20	.80
Totals	1472	802	.54

Table B   Numbers and Rates of Student Responses

Institution	Number of Questionnaires Returned Fall 1966	Number of Freshman Sample Still Enrolled in Spring 1970	Percentage of Freshman Sample Still Enrolled in Spring 1970	Number of Questionnaires Returned Spring 1970	Response Rate Spring 1970
University of California:					
Berkeley	2076	1157	.55	735	.64
Santa Cruz	213	122	.57	91	.75
Northeastern Illinois State College[a]	875	—		206	—
Monteith College	186	63	.34	29	.46
Luther College	498	319	.64	207	.65
University of the Pacific:					
College of the Pacific	416	178	.43	92	.52
Raymond College[b]	88	41	.47	50	.61
Clark College	291	114	.39	40	.35
Shimer College	172	45	.26	25	.56
Totals with Northeastern Illinois State College included	4815			1475	—
Totals with Northeastern Illinois State College excluded	3940	2078	.53	1279	.61

[a] Accurate records on the enrollment status of the students who entered in fall 1966 were not available in spring 1970, due in large part to the fact that enrollments doubled during the period of this study. Accordingly, the number or percentage of the freshmen who were still enrolled in spring, 1970 is not known, and a response rate cannot be calculated.

[b] Since this school has a three-year program, the senior data were gathered in spring 1969. Although only 25 of the students still enrolled in 1969 returned completed questionnaires, an additional 25 were obtained from students who had transferred. The response rate is based on the 25 of the 41 students who remained enrolled in this school.

DEVELOPMENT OF SCALES

For economy and efficiency in treating the data, eight scales were derived from the Faculty Questionnaire. To obtain the scales, 140 questionnaire items were subjected to a principal-components analysis with varimax rotation (Kaiser, 1958). The scales and the scale numbers are:

1. Discursiveness
2. Student Participation
3. Presentation Interest
4. Teaching Organization
5. Youth Culture Issues
6. Controversial Campus Issues
7. Personalization of Faculty–Student Relations
8. Self-Perceived Influence on Students

Table C Teaching Practices and Attitude Scales

Item Content	Varimax[a] Loading
1. Discursiveness	
Discuss the origins of ideas introduced in my class.	55
Invite student criticism of my ideas.	48
Discuss points of view other than my own.	46
Relate the course work to other fields of study.	46
Digress from prepared materials to pursue questions or comments from students.	42
Encourage students to discuss issues that go beyond class reading.	42
2. Student Participation	
Provide students with the opportunity to share their knowledge or experiences with the class.	73
Give students the responsibility for presenting topics, conducting panels, or leading class discussions.	72
Encourage students to get actively involved in the discussion.	59
Invite students to help make class plans or policy.	47
Allow time for student questions and discussion.	45
3. Presentation Interest	
Use stories and analogies to illuminate points that I make.	77
Tell humorous stories, anecdotes, and jokes.	74
Try to present materials in an entertaining way.	62
Use examples from my own experience or research.	61
Relate the course content to current social problems.	55
4. Teaching Organization	
Prepare and distribute a course outline at the beginning of the term.	68
Describe objectives at the beginning of the class session.	63
Lecture from detailed notes in class.	46
Summarize at the end of class the major points discussed.	45
5. Youth Culture Issues	
Below are a number of problems which young people today must confront. Please indicate the extent to which you have discussed each of them with students.	
The use of drugs.	78
Sex and morality.	77
Student activism or protest.	69
The draft.	68
Emerging life styles.	65
6. Controversial Campus Issues	
An avowed Communist was hired as a teacher.	75
Colleges should expel students who use the college as a base of operations for protest in the community.	−74

Table C   (Continued)

Item Content	Varimax[a] Loading
A student drama group performed a play on campus in which there was a nude scene.	71
A college has the right to set some rules regarding inappropriate attire on campus.	−66
Student body funds were used for bail loans to students arrested in a demonstration.	65
A faculty group called a work stoppage to hold mass meetings in protest of the war in Vietnam.	63
A faculty union called a strike.	61
College admission standards should be changed so that more minority students can be admitted.	61
The administration called police to evict students who had taken over a university building.	−54
A university gave student files to a legislative committee investigating campus unrest.	−51
7. Personalization of Faculty–Student Relations	
Students learn class material best if a teacher takes a personal interest in them.	67
It is a faculty member's responsibility to help students with personal problems they may bring him.	64
It is generally best for a faculty member to go out of his way to establish friendly relations with his students.	60
Informal out-of-class contacts with faculty members are an important part of a student's development.	52
A teacher can be effective without personally involving himself with his students.	−52
The emotional and personal development of a student should be as important to a teacher as his intellectual development.	49
8. Self-Perceived Influence on Students	
We are interested in learning from faculty members themselves how much impact they feel they have on students' lives. Of the students with whom you have contact, how much influence do you feel you have in helping them:	
Formulate their career plans?	73
Make decisions about their major field of study?	72
Acquire an appreciation of the values and methods of inquiry?	58
Develop their personal philosophy or outlook on life?	52

[a] Decimal omitted.

Table D   Intercorrelations of Teaching Practices and Attitude Scales[a]

Scale Number	1	2	3	4	5	6	7	8
1	76							
2	47	77						
3	53	32	78					
4	20	08	18	54				
5	31	28	22	04	87			
6	10	18	−01	−10	30	88		
7	18	31	18	05	28	10	72	
8	29	09	27	17	24	−17	16	77

$N = 802$

[a] Decimals omitted; diagonal values are Kuder-Richardson 21 reliabilities.

References

Arrowsmith, W. The future of teaching. In C. B. T. Lee (Ed.), *Improving College Teaching*. Washington, D.C.: American Council on Education, 1967.

Assembly on University Goals and Governance. *A first report*. Cambridge, Mass.: The American Academy of Arts and Sciences, 1971.

Astin, A. W., & Panos, R. J. *The educational and vocational development of college students*. Washington, D.C.: American Council on Education, 1969.

Bayer, A. E. *College and university faculty: A statistical description*. Washington, D.C.: American Council on Education, 1970.

Bayer, A. E. *Teaching faculty in Academe: 1972-73*. Washington, D.C.: American Council on Education, 1973.

Bess, J. L., & Bilorusky, J. L. Curriculum hypocrisies: Studies of student-initiated courses. *Universities Quarterly,* 1970, 24, 291-309.

Blackburn, R. T., & Linquist, J. D. Faculty behavior in the legislative process: Professorial attitudes versus behavior concerning the inclusion of students in academic decisionmaking. Unpublished manuscript. Ann Arbor: Center for the Study of Higher Education, University of Michigan, 1970.

Brick, M., & McGrath, E. J. *Innovation in liberal arts colleges*. New York: Teachers College Press, 1969.

Carnegie Commission on Higher Education. *Less time, more options: Education beyond the high school*. New York: McGraw-Hill, 1971.

Centra, J. A. *The student instructional report: Its development and uses*. SIR Report Number 1. Princeton, N.J.: Educational Testing Service, 1972a.

Centra, J. A. *The utility of student ratings for instructional improvement*. Princeton, N.J.: Educational Testing Service, 1972b.

Chickering, A. W. *Education and identity*. San Francisco: Jossey-Bass, 1969.

Christensen, P. R., Ruyle, J., & Hurst, J. *Characteristics of ethnic studies programs*. Berkeley: Center for Research and Development in Higher Education. University of California, 1971.

Clark, B. R., & Trow, M. *Determinants of college student subculture*. Berkeley: Center for Research and Development in Higher Education, University of California, 1960.

Clark, B. R., Heist, P., McConnell, T. R., Trow, M. A., & Yonge, G. *Students and colleges: Interaction and change*. Berkeley: Center for Research and Development in Higher Education, University of California, 1972.

Costin, F., Greenough, W., & Menges, R. Student rating of college teaching: Reliability, validity and usefulness. *Review of Educational Research,* 1971, **41,** 511-535.

Dienst, E. R. Psychological and activist political alienation related to faculty-student interaction. Unpublished doctoral dissertation, University of California, Berkeley, 1971.

Donohoe Higher Education Act, Section 22500 (Division 16.5), Education Code, State of California, 1960.

Dressel, P. L., & DeLisle, F. H.   *Undergraduate curriculum trends.* Washington, D.C.: American Council on Education, 1969.

Dubin, R., & Taveggia, T. C.   *The teaching–learning paradox: A comparative analysis of college teaching methods.* Eugene: Center for the Advanced Study of Educational Administration, University of Oregon, 1968.

Dunham, E. A.   *Colleges of the forgotten Americans.* New York: McGraw-Hill, 1969.

Dunham, R. E., Wright, P. S., & Chandler, M. O.   *Teaching faculty in universities and four-year colleges.* Washington, D.C.: U.S. Office of Education, 1966.

Eble, K. E.   *The recognition and evaluation of teaching.* Salt Lake City: Project to Improve College Teaching, 1970.

Eckert, R. E.   Participation in university policymaking: A second look. *AAUP Bulletin,* 1970, **56,** (3), 308–14.

Feldman, K. A., & Newcomb, T. M.   *The impact of college on students.* San Francisco: Jossey-Bass, 1969.

Freyman, J. M.   *The Occasional.* Exxon Education Foundation, December 1973.

Gaff, J. G., et al.   *The cluster college.* San Francisco: Jossey-Bass, 1970.

Gaff, J. G., & Wilson, R. C.   The teaching environment. *AAUP Bulletin,* 1971, **57,** (4), 475–493.

Gage, N. L.   *Handbook of research on teaching.* Chicago: Rand McNally, 1963.

Gamson, Z. F.   Utilitarian and normative orientation toward education. *Sociology of Education,* 1966, **39,** 46–73.

Gamson, Z. F.   Performance and personalism in student–faculty relations. *Sociology of Education,* 1967, **40,** 279–301.

Harcleroad, F. F., Sagen, H. B., & Molen, C. T., Jr.   *The developing state colleges and universities.* Iowa City: American College Testing Program, 1969.

Hayes, J. R.   Research, teaching, and faculty fate. *Science,* 1971, **172,** 227–230.

Hefferlin, J. B. L.   *Dynamics of academic reform.* San Francisco: Jossey-Bass, 1969.

Heiss, A. M.   *The preparation of college and university teachers.* Berkeley: Center for Research and Development in Higher Education, University of California, 1968.

Heist, P.   (Ed.)   *The creative college student: An unmet challenge.* San Francisco: Jossey-Bass, 1968.

Heist, P. & Yonge, G.   *Omnibus Personality Inventory Manual (Form F).* New York: The Psychological Corporation, 1968.

Heist, P. et al.   Longitudinal study of student development. Berkeley: Center for Research and Development in Higher Education, University of California. In preparation.

Heyns, R. W.   Berkeley: Yesterday, today and tomorrow. *Educational Record,* 1971, **52,** (3), 212–18.

Hildebrand, M., Wilson, R. C., & Dienst, E. R.   *Evaluating university teaching.* Berkeley: Center for Research and Development in Higher Education, University of California, 1971.

Hitch, C. J.   Instructions to appointment and promotion committees. *University Bulletin,* University of California, 1969, **18,** 30–32.

Hodgkinson, H. L. *Institutions in transition.* Berkeley: Carnegie Commission on Higher Education, 1970.

Holland, J. L. *The psychology of vocational choice.* Waltham, Mass.: Blaisdell, 1966.

Jacob, P. E. *Changing values in college: An exploratory study of the impact of college teaching.* New York: Harper, 1957.

Kaiser, H. F. The varimax criterion for analytic rotation in factor analysis. *Psychometrika,* 1958, **23,** 187–200.

Kampf, L. The scandal of literary scholarship. In T. Roszak (Ed.), *The dissenting academy.* New York: Pantheon, 1967.

Katz, E., & Lazarsfeld, P. F. *Personal influence.* New York: Free Press, 1955.

Keller, F. S. Good-bye, teacher. *Journal of Applied Behavior Analysis,* 1968, 1 (1), 79–89.

Kulik, J. A., Kulik, C. L., & Carmichael, K. The Keller plan in science teaching. *Science,* 1974, **183,** 379–383.

Lipset, S. M., & Ladd, E. C., Jr. The divided professoriate. *Change,* 1971, **3,** (3), 54–60.

Lunsford, T. F., & Duster, T. The student role in the authority system of higher education. In L. Deighton (Ed.), *Encyclopedia of Education.* New York: Crowell, Collier, & Macmillan, 1971.

McConnell, T. R. *The redistribution of power in higher education.* Berkeley: Center for Research and Development in Higher Education, University of California, 1971.

McConnell, T. R., & Mortimer, K. P. *The faculty in university governance.* Berkeley: Center for Research and Development in Higher Education, University of California, 1971.

McGee, R. *Academic Janus.* San Francisco: Jossey-Bass, 1971.

McHenry, D. E. *Chancellor's Memo.* University of California, Santa Cruz, July 1973.

McKeachie, W. J. New developments in teaching. *New Dimensions in Higher Education,* No. 16. Washington, D.C.: U.S. Department of Health, Education, and Welfare, 1967.

McKeachie, W. J. Student ratings of faculty. *AAUP Bulletin,* 1969, **55,** 439–44.

McKeachie, W. J. *Research on college teaching: A review.* Washington, D.C.: ERIC Clearinghouse on Higher Education, 1970.

Martin, W. B. *Conformity: Standards and change in higher education.* San Francisco: Jossey-Bass, 1969.

Medsker, L. L. *The junior college: Progress and prospect.* New York: McGraw-Hill, 1960.

Metsger, W. P. The crisis in academic authority. *Daedalus,* Summer 1970, **99,** 568–608.

Mortimer, K. P. *Academic governance at Berkeley.* Berkeley: Center for Research and Development in Higher Education, University of California, 1970.

Parsons, T., & Platt, G. M. *The American academic profession: A pilot study.* Cambridge, Mass.: Laboratory of Social Relations, Harvard University, 1968.

Peterson, R. E. *The scope of organized student protest in 1964–1965.* Princeton, N. J.: Educational Testing Service, 1966.

Peterson, R. E. *The scope of organized student protest in 1967–1968.* Princeton, N.J.: Educational Testing Service, 1969.

Remmers, H. H. The college professor as the student sees him. *Purdue University Studies in Higher Education,* 1929, **29,** 75.

Robinson, L. H., & Schoenfeld, J. D. *Student participation in academic governance.* Washington, D.C.: The George Washington University. ERIC Clearinghouse on Higher Education, Feb. 1970, 1.

Ryans, D. G. *Characteristics of teachers.* Washington, D.C.: American Council on Education, 1960.

Sanford, N. Academic culture and the teacher's development. Unpublished paper, Wright Institute, Berkeley, California, 1971.

Scott, J. W., & El-Assal, M. Multiversity, university size, university quality, and student protest: An empirical study. *American Sociological Review,* 1969, **34,** 702–09.

Snow, C. P. *The two cultures and the scientific revolution.* Cambridge, England: Cambridge University Press, 1959.

Sockloff, A. L. (Ed.) *Proceedings: The first invitational conference on faculty effectiveness as evaluated by students.* Philadelphia: Measurement and Research Center, Temple University, 1973.

Spaulding, C. B., & Turner, H. A. Political orientation and field of specialization among college professors. *Sociology of Education,* 1968, **41,** (3), 245–62.

Summerskill, J. Dropouts from college. In N. Sanford (Ed.), *The American college.* New York: Wiley, 1962.

Task Force on Academic Reform. *Report on higher education.* Washington, D.C.: U.S. Department of Health, Education, and Welfare, 1971.

Thielens, W. Jr. *The structure of faculty influence.* New York: The College Entrance Examination Board, Bureau of Applied Social Research, Columbia University, 1966.

Thielens, W., Jr. The teacher–student interaction, higher education: 2. Student viewpoint. In L. Deighton (Ed.), *Encyclopedia of Education.* New York: Crowell, Collier, & Macmillan, 1971, **9,** 54–63.

Thompson, J. D., Hawkes, R. W., & Avery, R. W. Truth strategies and university organization. *Educational Administration Quarterly,* 1969, **5,** (2), 4–25.

Travers, R. M. W. *Second handbook of research on teaching.* Chicago: Rand McNally, 1973.

Vreeland, R. S., & Bidwell, C. E. Classifying university departments: An approach to the analysis of their effects upon undergraduates' values and attitudes. *Sociology of Education,* 1966, **39,** 237–54.

Watts, W., & Whittaker, D. Free speech advocates at Berkeley. *Journal of Applied Behavioral Science,* 1966, **2,** (1), 41–62.

Wilson, R. C., Gaff, J. G., & Bavry, J. L. *Faculty characteristics questionnaire (Experimental Form 1) Manual of Information.* Berkeley: Center for Research and Development in Higher Education, University of California, 1970.

Index